BEAUTIES

OF

ENGLISH LANDSCAPE

DRAWN BY

BIRKET FOSTER

ENGRAVED BY

DALZIEL BROTHERS, J. COOPER, E. EVANS, H. HARRAL

AND OTHERS

LONDON AND NEW YORK

GEORGE ROUTLEDGE AND SONS

1874

ANNOUNCEMENT.

— ◆ —

IN producing this Book of Landscapes by BIRKET FOSTER, it is the intention of the Publishers to give in a collected form specimens of the works of this justly popular Artist, which have already appeared in their series of Illustrated Gift Books.

BROADWAY, LUDGATE.

CONTENTS AND ILLUSTRATIONS.

—◆— ---

CONTENTS AND ILLUSTRATIONS.

CONTENTS AND ILLUSTRATIONS.

xi

CONTENTS AND ILLUSTRATIONS.

xii

CONTENTS AND ILLUSTRATIONS.

CONTENTS AND ILLUSTRATIONS.

CONTENTS AND ILLUSTRATIONS.

SELECTIONS FROM BEATTIE'S "MINSTREL."

CONTENTS AND ILLUSTRATIONS.

A HOLY-DAY—the frugal banquet spread
On the fresh herbage near the fountain head,
With quips and cranks—what time the wood-lark there
Scatters her loose notes on the sultry air.

THE SUN.

MOST glorious art thou! when from thy pavilion
Thou lookest forth at morning; flinging wide
Its curtain clouds of purple and vermilion,
Dispensing life and light on every side;
Brightening the mountain cataract, dimly spied
Through glittering mist; opening each dew-gemm'd flower,
Or touching, in some hamlet, far descried,
Its spiral wreaths of smoke that upward tower,
Where birds their matin sing from many a leafy bower.

And more magnificent art thou, bright Sun!
Uprising from the Ocean's billowy bed:
Who that has seen thee thus, as I have done,
Can e'er forget the effulgent splendours spread
From thy emerging radiance? Upward sped,
Even to the centre of the vaulted sky,
Thy beams pervade the heavens, and o'er them shed
Hues indescribable—of gorgeous dye,
Making among the clouds mute glorious pageantry.

Then, then how beautiful across the deep
The lustre of thy orient path of light!
Onward, still onward, o'er the waves that leap
So lovelily, and show their crests of white,
The eye, unsated in its own despite,
Still up that vista gazes; till thy way
Over the waters seems a pathway bright
For holiest thoughts to travel, there to pay
Man's homage unto Him who bade thee "rule the Day."

BARTON.

2

WILD FLOWERS.

A FILBERT-EDGE with wild-brier overtwined,
And clumps of woodbine taking the soft wind
Upon their summer thrones; there too should be
The frequent checker of a youngling tree,
That with a score of bright-green brethren shoots
From the quaint mossiness of aged roots:
Round which is heard a spring head of clear waters,
Prattling so wildly of its lovely daughters,
The spreading bluebells: it may haply mourn
That such fair clusters should be rudely torn
From their fresh beds, and scatter'd thoughtlessly
By infant hands, left on the path to die.
Open afresh your round of starry folds,
Ye ardent marigolds!
Dry up the moisture from your golden lids,
For great Apollo bids
That in these days your praises should be sung
On many harps, which he has lately strung;
And when again your dewiness he kisses,
Tell him, I have you in my world of blisses:
So haply when I rove in some far vale,
His mighty voice may come upon the gale.
    Here are sweet-peas, on tip-toe for a flight,
With wings of gentle flush o'er delicate white,
And taper fingers catching at all things,
To bind them all about with tiny rings.
What next? A turf of evening primroses,
O'er which the mind may hover till it dozes;
O'er which it well might take a pleasant sleep,
But that 't is ever startled by the leap
Of buds into ripe flowers.

KEATS.

LABURNUM, rich
In streaming gold; syringa, iv'ry pure;
The scentless and the scented rose: this red,
And of an humbler growth, the other, tall,
And throwing up into the darkest gloom
Of neighb'ring cypress, or more sable yew,
Her silver globes, light as the foamy surf
That the wind severs from the broken wave.
The lilac, various in array, now white,
Now sanguine, and her beauteous head now set
With purple spikes pyramidal, as if,
Studious of ornament, yet unresolved
Which hue she most approved, she chose them all;
Copious of flowers the woodbine, pale and wan,
But well compensating her sickly looks
With never-cloying odours, early and late.

COWPER.

MY SISTER ELLEN.

SISTER ELLEN, I've been dreaming
  Of a fair and happy time;
Gentle thoughts are round me gleaming,
  Thoughts of sunny girlhood's prime:
Oh, the light, untutored fancies,
  Images so quaint and bold—
Outlines dim of old romances,
  Forming childhood's age of gold!
Eternal spring was then above us,
  Sunshine cheered our every path;
None then knew us but to love us—
  Winning ways sweet childhood hath.

Thou art little Nelly, looking
  Up into my anxious face,
I thy childish caprice brooking,
  As thy merry thoughts I trace:
See thy dreamy blue eyes glancing
  From thy founts of light and glee,
And thy little feet go dancing
  Like the waves upon the sea!
Tossing from thy snowy shoulder
  Golden curls with witching grace,
Charming every new beholder
  With thine arch, expressive face.

Sister Ellen! I've been dreaming
  Of some lightsome summer eves,
When the harvest-moon was beaming
  Softly through the dewy leaves—
How among the flowers we wandered,
  Treading light as summer air;
Looking upward, how we pondered
  On the dazzling glories there!
We were children then together,
  Though I older was in years,
And life's dark and stormy weather
  Seemed like April's smiles and tears.

REBECCA S. NICHOLS.

8

THEN, as I wandered where the huddling rill
Brightens with water-breaks the hollow ghyll,*
To where, while thick above the branches close,
In dark brown bason its wild waves repose,
Inverted shrubs, and moss of darkest green,
Cling from the rocks, with pale wood-weeds between ;
Save that aloft the subtle sunbeams shine
On withered briars that o'er the crags recline ;
Sole light admitted here, a small cascade
Illumes with sparkling from the twilight shade ;
Beyond, along the vista of the brook,
Where antique roots its bustling path o'erlook,
The eye reposes on a secret bridge
Half grey, half shagged with ivy to its ridge.

Sweet Rill, farewell ! To morrow's noon again
Shall hide me, wooing long thy wildwood strain ;
But now the sun has gained his western road,
And eve's mild hour invites my steps abroad.

WORDSWORTH.

* *Ghyll*, dingle.

THE HAMLET.

THE hinds how blest, who ne'er beguiled
To quit their hamlet's hawthorn wild,
Nor haunt the crowd, nor tempt the main,
For splendid care and guilty gain !

When morning's twilight-tinctured beam
Strikes their low thatch with slanting gleam
They rove abroad in ether blue,
To dip the scythe in fragrant dew ;
The sheaf to bind, the beech to fell,
That nodding shades a craggy dell.

'Midst gloomy glades, in warbles clear,
Wild Nature's sweetest notes they hear :
On green untrodden banks they view
The hyacinth's neglected hue ;
In their lone haunts, and woodland rounds,
They spy the squirrel's airy bounds ;
And startle from her ashen spray,
Across the glen, the screaming jay :
Each native charm their steps explore
Of solitude's sequester'd store.

For them the moon with cloudless ray
Mounts, to illume their homeward way :
Their weary spirits to relieve,
The meadows incense breathe at eve.
No riot mars the simple fare
That o'er a glimmering hearth they share :

But when the curfew's measured roar
Duly, the darkening valleys o'er,
Has echoed from the distant town,
They wish no beds of cygnet-down,
No trophied canopies, to close
Their drooping eyes in quick repose.

Their little sons, who spread the bloom
Of health around the clay-built room,
Or through the primrosed coppice stray,
Or gambol in the new-mown hay ;
Or quaintly braid the cowslip-twine,
Or drive afield the tardy kine ;
Or hasten from the sultry hill,
To loiter at the shady rill ;
Or climb the tall pine's gloomy crest,
To rob the raven's ancient nest.

Their humble porch with honey'd flowers
The curling woodbine's shade embowers ;
From the small garden's thymy mound
Their bees in busy swarms resound ;
Nor fell Disease, before his time,
Hastes to consume life's golden prime.
But when their temples long have wore
The silver crown of tresses hoar,
As studious still calm peace to keep,
Beneath a flowery turf they sleep.

WARTON.

12

A NARROW girdle of rough stones and crags,
A rude and natural causeway, interposed
Between the water and a winding slope
Of copse and thicket, leaves the eastern shore
Of Grasmere safe in its own privacy;
And there myself and two belovèd Friends,
One calm September morning, ere the mist
Had altogether yielded to the sun,
Sauntered on this retired and difficult way.

Ill suits the road with one in haste, but we
Played with our time; and, as we strolled along,
It was our occupation to observe
Such objects as the waves had tossed ashore—
Feather, or leaf, or weed, or withered bough,
Each on the other heaped, along the line
Of the dry wreck. And, in our vacant mood,
Not seldom did we stop to watch some tuft
Of dandelion seed or thistle's beard,
That skimmed the surface of the dead calm lake.
Suddenly halting now—a lifeless stand!
And starting off again with freak as sudden;
In all its sportive wanderings, all the while,
Making report of an invisible breeze
That was its wings, its chariot, and its horse,
Its very playmate and its moving soul.

WORDSWORTH.

NEST OF THE NIGHTINGALE.

Up this green woodland side let's softly rove,
And list the nightingale; she dwells just here.
Hush! let the wood-gate softly clap, for fear
The noise might drive her from her home of love;
For here I've heard her many a merry year—
At morn, at eve—nay, all the live-long day,
As though she lived on song. This very spot,
Just where the old-man's-beard all wildly trails
Rude arbours o'er the road, and stops the way;
And where the child its blue-bell flowers hath got,
Laughing and creeping through the mossy rails;
There have I hunted like a very boy,
Creeping on hands and knees through matted thorn,
To find her nest, and see her feed her young,
And vainly did I many hours employ:
All seem'd as hidden as a thought unborn;
And where those crumpling fern-leaves ramp among
The hazel's under-boughs, I've nestled down
And watch'd her while she sang; and her renown
Hath made me marvel that so famed a bird
Should have no better dress than russet brown.
Her wings would tremble in her ecstasy,
And feathers stand on end, as 'twere with joy;
And mouth wide open to release her heart
Of its out-sobbing songs. The happiest part
Of summer's fame she shared, for so to me
Did happy fancy shapen her employ.
But if I touch'd a bush, or scarcely stirr'd,
All in a moment stopt. I watch'd in vain:
The timid bird had left the hazel-bush,
And oft in distance hid to sing again.

                                        CLARE.

16

LINES WRITTEN IN EARLY SPRING.

I HEARD a thousand blended notes,
While in the grove I sat reclin'd,
In that sweet mood when pleasant thoughts
Bring sad thoughts to the mind.

To her fair works did Nature link
The human soul that through me ran;
And much it grieved my heart to think
What man has made of man.

Through primrose tufts, in that sweet bower,
The periwinkle trailed its wreaths;
And 't is my faith that every flower
Enjoys the air it breathes.

The birds around me hopped and play'd
Their thoughts I cannot measure :—
But the least motion which they made,
It seemed a thrill of pleasure.

The budding twigs spread out their fan,
To catch the breezy air;
And I must think, do all I can,
That there was pleasure there.

If I these thoughts may not prevent,
If such be of my creed the plan,
Have I not reason to lament
What man has made of man?

WORDSWORTH.

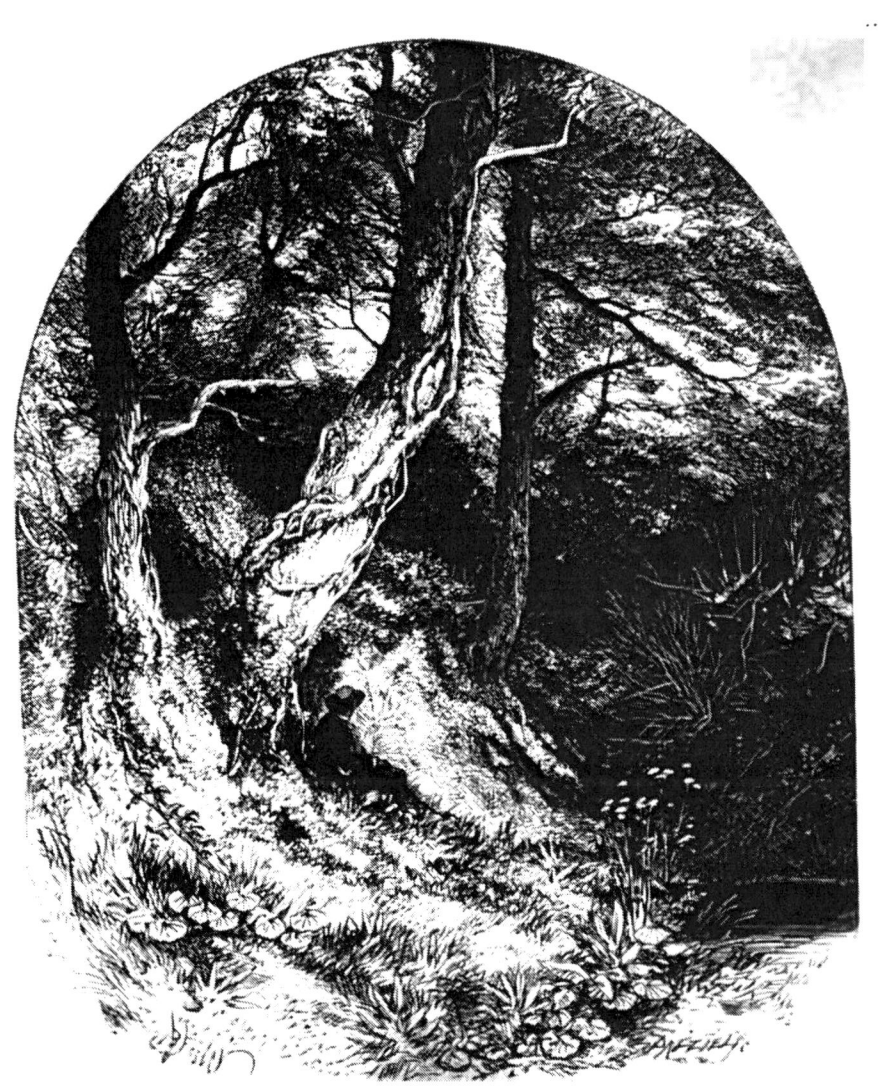

DOMESTIC LOVE.

DOMESTIC LOVE ! not in proud palace halls
Is often seen thy beauty to abide ;
Thy dwelling is in lowly cottage walls,
That in the thickets of the woodbine hide ;
With hum of bees around, and from the side
Of woody hills some little bubbling spring,
Shining along through banks with harebells dyed ;
And many a bird to warble on the wing,
When Morn her saffron robe o'er heaven and earth doth fling.

O ! love of loves !—to thy white hand is given
Of earthly happiness the golden key !
Thine are the joyous hours of winter's even,
When the babes cling around their father's knee ;
And thine the voice, that on the midnight sea
Melts the rude mariner with thoughts of home,
Peopling the gloom with all he longs to see.
Spirit !—I 've built a shrine ; and thou hast come,
And on its altar closed—for ever closed thy plume !

GEORGE CROLY

LINES

LEFT UPON A SEAT IN A YEW-TREE, WHICH STANDS NEAR THE LAKE OF ESTHWAITE, ON A DESOLATE PART OF THE SHORE, COMMANDING A BEAUTIFUL PROSPECT.

NAY, traveller! rest. This lonely Yew-tree stands
Far from human dwelling: what if here
No sparkling rivulet spread the verdant herb?
What if these barren boughs the bee not loves?
Yet, if the wind breathe soft, the curling waves,
That break against the shore, shall lull thy mind
By one soft impulse saved from vacancy.
                                   Who he was
That piled these stones and with the mossy sod
First covered o'er, and taught this aged Tree
With its dark arms to form a circling bower,
I well remember.—He was one who owned
No common soul. In youth by Science nursed,
And led by Nature into a wild scene
Of lofty hopes, he to the world went forth
A favoured being, knowing no desire
Which genius did not hallow;—'gainst the taint
Of dissolute tongues, and jealousy, and hate,
And scorn,—against all enemies prepared,
All but neglect. The world, for so it thought,
Owed him no service: wherefore he at once
With indignation turned himself away,
And with the food of pride sustained his soul
In solitude.—Stranger! these gloomy boughs
Had charms for him; and here he loved to sit,
His only visitants a straggling sheep,
The stone-chat, or the sand-lark, restless bird,
Piping along the margin of the lake.
And on these barren rocks, with juniper,
And heath, and thistle, thinly sprinkled o'er,
Fixing his downcast eye, he many an hour
A morbid pleasure nourished, tracing here
An emblem of his own unfruitful life:
And, lifting up his head, he then would gaze
On the more distant scene,—how lovely 't is
Thou seest,—and he would gaze till it became
Far lovelier, and his heart could not sustain
The beauty, still more beauteous! Nor, that time,
When Nature had subdued him to herself,
Would he forget those beings, to whose minds,
Warm from the labours of benevolence,
The world, and man himself, appeared a scene
Of kindred loveliness: then he would sigh
With mournful joy, to think that others felt

What he must never feel: and so, lost man!
On visionary views would fancy feed,
Till his eye streamed with tears.   In this deep vale
He died,—this seat his only monument.
   If thou be one whose heart the holy forms
Of young imagination have kept pure,
Stranger! henceforth be warned; and know that pride,
Howe'er disguised in his own majesty,
Is littleness; that he who feels contempt
For any living thing, hath faculties
Which he has never used; that thought with him
Is in its infancy.   The man whose eye
Is ever on himself, doth look on one,
The least of Nature's works, one who might move
The wise man to that scorn which wisdom holds
Unlawful, ever.   O be wiser, thou!
Instructed that true knowledge leads to love;
True dignity abides with him alone
Who, in the silent hour of inward thought,
Can still suspect, and still revere himself,
In lowliness of heart.
WORDSWORTH.

Now, with religious awe, the farewell light
Blends with the solemn colouring of night ;
'Mid groves of clouds that crest the mountain's brow,
And round the west's proud lodge their shadows throw,
Like Una shining on her gloomy way.
The half-seen form of Twilight roams astray ;
Shedding, through paly loopholes, mild and small,
Gleams that upon the lake's still bosom fall ;
Soft o'er the surface creep those lustres pale,
Tracking the fitful motions of the gale.
With restless interchange at once the bright
Wins on the shade, the shade upon the light.
No favoured eye was e'er allowed to gaze
On lovelier spectacle in fairy days ;
When gentle Spirits urged a sportive chase,
Brushing with lucid wands the water's face.
While music, stealing round the glimmering deeps,
Charmed the tall circle of the enchanted steeps.

WORDSWORTH.

'T is list'ning fear and dumb amazement all :
When to the startled eye the sudden glance
Appears far south, eruptive through the cloud ;
And following slower, in explosion vast,
The thunder raises his tremendous voice.
At first heard solemn o'er the verge of heaven,
The tempest growls ; but as it nearer comes
And rolls its awful burden on the wind,
The lightnings flash a larger curve, and more
The noise astounds ; till overhead a sheet
Of livid flame discloses wide ; then shuts,
And opens wider ; shuts and opens still
Expansive, wrapping æther in a blaze :
Follows the loosen'd aggravated roar,
Enlarging, deep'ning, mingling, peal on peal
Crush'd horrible, convulsive heav'n and earth.

THOMSON.

THE BROTHERS.

THE homely Priest of Ennerdale.
It was a July evening; and he sate
Upon the long stone seat beneath the eaves
Of his old cottage.   .   .   .   .
    .   .   .   .   Upon the stone
His wife sat near him, teasing matted wool.
    .   .   .   .   Towards the field
In which the Parish Chapel stood alone,
Girt round with a bare ring of mossy wall,
While half an hour went by, the Priest had sent
Many a long look of wonder; and at last,
Risen from his seat, beside the snow-white ridge
Of carded wool which the old man had piled,
He laid his implements with gentle care,
Each in the other locked; and down the path

Which from his cottage to the Church-yard led,
He took his way, impatient to accost
The Stranger, whom he saw still lingering there.

"'T was one well known to him in former days,
A shepherd lad;—who ere his sixteenth year
Had left that calling, tempted to entrust
His expectations to the fickle winds
And perilous waters; with the mariners
A fellow-mariner,—and so had fared
Through twenty seasons. . . . .
            And now at last,
From perils manifold, with some small wealth
Acquired by traffic in the Indian Isles,

To his paternal home he is returned,
With a determined purpose to resume
The life which he lived there ; both for the sake
Of many darling pleasures, and the love
Which to an only Brother he has borne
In all his hardships. . . . .
Towards the Church-yard he had turned aside,—
That, as he knew in what particular spot
His family were laid, he thence might learn
If still his brother lived, or to the file
Another grave was added. . . . . .
   By this the Priest, who down the field had come,
Unseen by Leonard, at the Church-yard gate
Stopped short. . . . .
. . . . The Stranger, who had left the grave,
Approached ; he recognized the Priest at once,
And, after greetings interchanged, and given
By Leonard to the Vicar as to one
Unknown to him, this dialogue ensued.

PRIEST.

              Orphans !—Such they were—
Yet not while Walter lived :—for, though their parents
Lay buried side by side as now they lie,
The old man was a father to the boys,
Two fathers in one father. . . . . . .

LEONARD.

              These boys—I hope
They loved this good old man ?

PRIEST.

              They did—and truly :
But that was what we almost overlooked,
They were such darlings of each other. . . .
. . . . From their house the school
Was distant three short miles—and in the time
Of storm and thaw, when every water-course

And unbridged stream, such as you may have noticed
Crossing our roads at every hundred steps,
Was swoln into a noisy rivulet,
Would Leonard then, when elder boys perhaps

Remained at home, go staggering through the fords
Bearing his Brother on his back. I 've seen him,
On windy days, in one of those stray brooks,
Ay, more than once I 've seen him, mid-leg deep,
Their two books lying both on a dry stone
Upon the hither side. . . . .

LEONARD.

It seems, these Brothers have not lived to be
A comfort to each other.—

PRIEST.

                That they might
Live to such end, is what both old and young
In this our valley, all of us have wished,
And what, for my part, I have often prayed :
But Leonard— . . . .
. . . . . Poor Leonard ! when we parted,
He took me by the hand and said to me,
If ever the day came when he was rich,
He would return, and on his father's land
He would grow old among us.

LEONARD.

You said his kindred all were in their graves,
And that he had one Brother—

PRIEST.

                  That is but
A fellow-tale of sorrow. From his youth
James, though not sickly, yet was delicate :
. . . . And, when his Brother
Was gone to sea, and he was left alone,
The little colour that he had was soon
Stolen from his cheek ; he drooped, and pined, and pined.

LEONARD.

              But this youth,
How did he die at last?

THE BROTHERS.

PRIEST.

You see yon precipice ;—it almost looks
Like some vast building made of many crags ;
And in the midst is one particular rock
That rises like a column from the vale.
They found him at the foot of that same rock
Dead, and with mangled limbs. The third day after
I buried him, poor youth, and there he lies !
. . . . We all conjectured
That, as the day was warm, he had lain down
Upon the grass,—and, waiting for his comrades,
He there had fallen asleep ; that in his sleep
He to the margin of the precipice
Had walked, and from the **summit had** fallen headlong ;
And so no doubt he perished. . . . . . .

And Leonard, when they reached the Church-yard gate,
As the Priest lifted up the latch, turned round,—
And, looking at the grave, he said, "My Brother."

WORDSWORTH.

THE VILLAGE INN.

NEAR yonder thorn that lifts its head on high,
Where once the sign-post caught the passing eye,
Low lies that house where nut-brown draughts inspired,
Where greybeard mirth and smiling toil retired,
Where village statesmen talk'd with looks profound,
And news much older than their ale went round.
Imagination fondly stoops to trace
The parlour splendours of that festive place;
The whitewash'd wall, the nicely sanded floor,
The varnish'd clock that click'd behind the door;
The chest contrived a double debt to pay,
A bed by night, a chest of drawers by day;
The pictures placed for ornament and use,
The twelve good rules, the royal game of goose;
The hearth, except when winter chill'd the day,
With aspen boughs, and flowers, and fennel gay;
While broken tea-cups, wisely kept for show,
Ranged o'er the chimney, glisten'd in a row.

GOLDSMITH.

Upon a hill
At a short distance from my cottage, stands
A stately Fir-grove, whither I was wont
To hasten, for I found, beneath the roof
Of that perennial shade, a cloistral place
Of refuge, with an unencumbered floor.

WORDSWORTH.

DOMESTIC PEACE.

TELL me, on what holy ground
May Domestic Peace be found?
Halcyon Daughter of the skies,
Far on fearful wings she flies,
From the pomp of sceptred state,
From the Rebel's noisy hate.
In a cottaged vale she dwells,
Listening to the Sabbath bells!
Still around her steps are seen
Spotless Honour's meeker mien,
Love, the sire of pleasing fears,
Sorrow smiling through her tears,
And, conscious of the past employ,
Memory, bosom-spring of joy.

COLERIDGE.

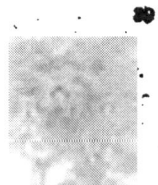

HUNG o'er a cloud above the steep that rears,
Its edge all flame, the broadening sun appears;
A long blue bar its ægis orb divides,
And breaks the spreading of its golden tides;
And now it touches on the purple steep
That flings its shadow on the pictured deep.
'Cross the calm lake's blue shades the cliffs aspire,
With towers and woods, a "prospect all on fire;"
The coves and secret hollows, through a ray
Of fainter gold, a purple gleam betray.
The gilded turf arrays in richer green
Each speck of lawn the broken rocks between:
Deep yellow beams the scattered boles illume,
Far in the level forest's central gloom:
Waving his hat, the shepherd, in the vale,
Directs his winding dog the cliffs to scale,—
That barking, busy 'mid the glittering rocks,
Hunts, where he points, the intercepted flocks.
Where oaks o'erhang the road, the radiance shoots
On tawny earth, wild weeds, and twisted roots;
The druid-stones their lighted fane enfold;
And all the babbling brooks are liquid gold;
Sunk to a curve, the day-star lessens still,
Gives one bright glance, and drops behind the hill.*

WORDSWORTH

* From Thomson.

LOVE.

I.

WE met in secret, in the depth of night
When there was none to watch us ; not an eye
Save the lone dweller of the lonely sky
To gaze upon our love and pure delight ;
And in that hour's unbroken solitude,
When the white moon had robed her in its beam,
I 've thought some vision of a blessed dream,
Or spirit of the air before me stood,
And held communion with me. In mine ear
Her voice's sweet notes breathed not of the earth,
Her beauty seemed not of a mortal birth ;
And in my heart there was an awful fear,
A thrill, like some deep warning from above,
That soothed its passion to a spirit's love.

II.

SHE stood before me ; the pure lamps of heaven
Lighted her charms, and those soft eyes which turned
On me with dying fondness. My heart burned,
As, tremblingly with hers, my vows were given.
Then softly 'gainst my bosom beat her heart ;
These living arms around her form were thrown,
Binding her heavenly beauty like a zone,
While from her ruby warm lips, just apart
Like bursting roses, sighs of fragrance stole,
And words of music whispering in mine ear
Things pure and holy none but mine should hear ;
For they were accents uttered from the soul,
For which no tongue her innocence reproved,
And breathed for one who loved her and was loved.

ISMAEL FITZADAM.

42

WOODS IN WINTER.

WHEN winter winds are piercing chill,
  And through the hawthorn blows the gale,
With solemn feet I tread the hill
  That overbrows the lonely vale.

O'er the bare upland, and away
  Through the long reach of desert woods,
The embracing sunbeams chastely play,
  And gladden those deep solitudes

Where, twisted round the barren oak,
  The summer vine in beauty clung,
And summer winds the silence broke,
  The crystal icicle is hung ;

Where, from their frozen urns, mute springs
  Pour out the river's gradual tide,
Shrilly the skater's iron rings,
  And voices fill the woodland side.

Alas ! how changed from the fair scene,
  When birds sang out their mellow lay,
And winds were soft, and woods were green,
  And the song ceased not with the day.

But still wild music is abroad,
  Pale, desert woods ! within your crowd ;
And gathering winds in hoarse accord
  Amid the vocal reeds pipe loud.

Chill airs, and wintry winds ! my ear
  Has grown familiar with your song ;
I hear it in the opening year—
  I listen, and it cheers me long.

LONGFELLOW.

It was in truth a lamentable hour
When from the last hill-top my sire surveyed,
Peering above the trees, the steeple tower
That on his marriage-day sweet music made!
Till then he hoped his bones might there be laid
Close by my mother in their native bowers;
Bidding me trust in God, he stood and prayed;—
I could not pray:—through tears that fell in showers
I saw my own dear home, that was no longer ours.

WORDSWORTH.

YEW-TREES.

THERE is a Yew-tree, pride of Lorton Vale,
Which to this day stands single, in the midst
Of its own darkness, as it stood of yore:
Not loth to furnish weapons for the bands
Of Umfraville or Percy, ere they marched
To Scotland's heaths; or those that crossed the sea
And drew their sounding bows at Azincour,
Perhaps at earlier Crecy, or Poictiers.
Of vast circumference and gloom profound
This solitary tree!—a living thing
Produced too slowly ever to decay;
Of form and aspect too magnificent
To be destroyed. But worthier still of note
Are those fraternal Four of Borrowdale,
Joined in one solemn and capacious grove;
Huge trunks!—and each particular trunk a growth
Of intertwisted fibres serpentine
Upcoiling, and inveterately convolved;
Nor uninformed with Phantasy, and looks
That threaten the profane; a pillared shade,
Upon whose grassless floor of red-brown hue,
By sheddings from the pining umbrage tinged
Perennially—beneath whose sable roof
Of boughs, as if for festal purpose, decked
With unrejoicing berries—ghostly Shapes
May meet at noontide—Fear and trembling Hope,
Silence and Foresight—Death the Skeleton
And Time the Shadow—there to celebrate,
As in a natural temple scattered o'er
With altars undisturbed of mossy stone,
United worship; or in mute repose
To lie, and listen to the mountain flood
Murmuring from Glaramara's inmost caves.

WORDSWORTH.

FAR from my dearest Friend, 't is mine to rove
Through bare grey dell, high wood, and pastoral cove ;
His wizard course where hoary Derwent takes,
Through crags and forest glooms and opening lakes,
Staying his silent waves, to hear the roar
That stuns the tremulous cliffs of high Lodore ;
Where peace to Grasmere's lonely island leads,
To willowy hedge rows, and to emerald meads ;
Leads to her bridge, rude church, and cottaged grounds,
Her rocky sheep-walks, and her woodland bounds ;
Where, bosomed deep, the shy Winander peeps
'Mid clustering isles, and holly-sprinkled steeps ;
Where twilight glens endear my Esthwaite's shore,
And memory of departed pleasures, more.

WORDSWORTH.

CHRISTMAS IN THE OLDEN TIME.

HEAP on more wood!—the wind is chill:
But let it whistle as it will,
We'll keep our Christmas merry still.
Each age has deem'd the new-born year
The fittest time for festal cheer;
And well our Christian sires of old
Loved when the year its course had roll'd,
And brought blithe Christmas back again,
With all his hospitable train.
Domestic and religious rite
Gave honour to the holy night:
On Christmas Eve the bells were rung;
On Christmas Eve the mass was sung.
That only night, in all the year,
Saw the stoled priest the chalice rear.
The damsel donn'd her kirtle sheen;
The hall was dress'd with holly green;
Forth to the wood did merry men go,
To gather in the mistletoe;
Then open'd wide the baron's hall
To vassal, tenant, serf, and all;
Power laid his rod of rule aside,
And Ceremony doff'd his pride.
The heir, with roses in his shoes,
That night might village partner choose;
The lord, underogating, share
The vulgar game of "post and pair."
All hail'd, with uncontroll'd delight,
And general voice, the happy night,
That to the cottage, as the crown,
Brought tidings of salvation down.
The fire, with well-dried logs supplied,
Went roaring up the chimney wide;
The huge hall table's oaken face,

Scrubb'd till it shone, the day to grace,
Bore then upon its massive board
No mark to part the squire and lord.
Then was brought in the lusty brawn
By old blue-coated serving-man;
Then the grim boar's head frown'd on high,
Crested with bays and rosemary.
Well can the green-garbed ranger tell
How, when, and where the monster fell;
What dogs before his death he tore,
And all the baiting of the boar.
The wassail round, in good brown bowls,
Garnish'd with ribbons, blithely trowls.
There the huge sirloin reek'd; hard by
Plum-porridge stood, and Christmas pie;
Nor fail'd old Scotland to produce,
At such high tide, her savoury goose.
Then came the merry masquers in,
And carols roar'd with blithesome din;
If unmelodious was the song,
It was a hearty note, and strong,—
Who lists may in their mumming see
Traces of ancient mystery.
White shirts supplied the masquerade,
And smutted cheeks the visors made;
But, oh! what masquers, richly dight,
Can boast of bosoms half so light!
England was merry England, when
Old Christmas brought his sports again.
'Twas Christmas broach'd the mightiest ale;
'Twas Christmas told the merriest tale;
A Christmas gambol oft could cheer
The poor man's heart through half the year.

SCOTT.

THE WORLD WITH US.

THE world is too much with us; late and soon,
   Getting and spending we lay waste our powers:
   Little we see in Nature that is ours;
We have given our hearts away, a sordid boon!

This sea that bares her bosom to the moon;
   The winds that will be howling at all hours
   And are up-gathered now like sleeping flowers;
For this, for everything, we are out of tune;

It moves us not.—Great God! I'd rather be
   A Pagan suckled in a creed outworn;
So might I, standing on this pleasant lea,
   Have glimpses that would make me less forlorn;
Have sight of Proteus coming from the sea,
   Or hear old Triton blow his wreathèd horn.

WORDSWORTH.

CYTHNA.

SHE moved upon this earth a shape of brightness,
A power, that from its objects scarcely drew
One impulse of her being—in her lightness
Most like some radiant cloud of morning dew,
Which wanders through the waste air's pathless blue
To nourish some far desert; she did seem
Beside me, gathering beauty as she grew,
Like the bright shade of some immortal dream
Which walks, when tempest sleeps, the wave of life's dark stream.

As mine own shadow was this child to me,
A second self, far dearer and more fair,
Which clothed in undissolving radiancy
All those steep paths which languor and despair
Of human things had made so dark and bare,
But which I trod alone, nor, till bereft
Of friends, and overcome by lonely care,
Knew I what solace for that loss was left,
Though by a bitter wound my trusting heart was cleft.

Once she was dear, now she was all I had
To love in human life, this playmate sweet,
This child of twelve years old, so she was made
My sole associate, and her willing feet
Wandered with mine, where earth and ocean meet
Beyond the aërial mountains, whose vast cells
The unreposing billows ever beat.
Through forests wide and old, and lowing dells,
Where boughs of incense droop over the emerald wells.

And warm and light I felt her clasping hand,
When twined in mine; she followed where I went
Through the lone paths of our immortal land,
It had no waste, but some memorial lent
Which strung me to my toil—some monument
Vital with mind—then Cythna by my side,
Until the bright and beaming hours were spent,
Would rest with looks entreating to abide
Too earnest, and too sweet ever to be denied.

And soon I could not have refused her—thus
For ever, day and night; we two were ne'er
Parted, but when brief sleep divided us,
And when the pauses of the lulling air
Of noon beside the sea had made a lair
For her soothed senses, in my arms she slept;
And I kept watch over her slumbers there,
While, as the shifting visions over her swept,
Amid her innocent rest by turns she smiled and wept.

SHELLEY.

THE coot was swimming in the reedy pond
  Beside the water-hen, so soon affrighted;
And in the weedy moat the heron, fond
  Of solitude, alighted.

The moping heron, motionless and stiff,
  That on a stone as silently and slyly
Stood an apparent sentinel, as if
  To guard the water-lily.

HOOD.

AUTUMN.

SEASON of mists and mellow fruitfulness!
  Close bosom-friend of the maturing sun;
Conspiring with him how to load and bless
  With fruit the vines that round the thatch-eaves run;
To bend with apples the moss'd cottage trees,
  And fill all fruit with ripeness to the core;
    To swell the gourd and plump the hazel-shells
  With a sweet kernel; to set budding more,
And still more, later flowers for the bees,
Until they think warm days will never cease,
    For summer has o'er-brimm'd their clammy cells.

Who hath not seen thee oft amid thy store?
  Sometimes, whoever seeks abroad may find
Thee sitting careless on a granary floor,
  Thy hair soft-lifted by the winnowing wind;
Or on a half-reap'd furrow sound asleep,
  Drowsed with the fume of poppies, while thy hook
    Spares the next swath and all its twinèd flowers;
And sometimes like a gleaner thou dost keep
  Steady thy laden head across a brook;
  Or by a cider-press, with patient look,
    Thou watchest the last oozings, hours by hours.

Where are the songs of Spring? Ay, where are they?
  Think not of them, thou hast thy music too,
While barred clouds bloom the soft dying day,
  And touch the stubble-plains with rosy hue;
Then in a wailful choir the small gnats mourn
  Among the river sallows, borne aloft
    Or sinking as the light wind lives or dies;
And full-grown lambs loud bleat from hilly bourn;
  Hedge-crickets sing; and now with treble soft
  The redbreast whistles from a garden croft,
    And gathering swallows twitter in the skies.

KEATS.

60

My heart leaps up when I behold
   A rainbow in the sky:
So was it when my life began;
So is it now I am a man;
So be it when I shall grow old,
   Or let me die!
The child is father of the man;
And I could wish my days to be
Bound each to each by natural piety.

WORDSWORTH.

CANST THOU FORGET?

CANST thou forget, beloved, our first awaking
 From out the shadowy calms of doubts and dreams,
To know Love's perfect sunlight round us breaking,
 Bathing our beings in its gorgeous gleams— .
       Canst thou forget?

A sky of rose and gold was o'er us glowing,
 Around us was the morning breath of May;
Then met our soul-tides, thence together flowing,
 Then kissed our thought-waves, mingling on their way:
       Canst thou forget?

Canst thou forget when first thy loving fingers
 Laid gently back the locks upon my brow?
Ah, to my woman's thought that touch still lingers
 And softly glides along my forehead now!
       Canst thou forget?

Canst thou forget when every twilight tender,
 'Mid dews and sweets, beheld our slow steps rove,
And when the nights, which come in starry splendour,
 Seemed dim and pallid to our heaven of love?
       Canst thou forget?

Canst thou forget the childlike heart-outpouring
 Of her whose fond faith knew no faltering fears?
The lashes drooped to veil her eyes' adoring,
 Her speaking silence, and her blissful tears?
       Canst thou forget?

Canst thou forget the last most mournful meeting,
 The trembling form clasped to thine anguished breast;
The heart against thine own, now wildly beating,
 Now fluttering faint, grief-wrung, and fear-oppress'd—
       Canst thou forget?

Canst thou forget, though all Love's spells be broken,
  The wild farewell, which rent our souls apart?
And that last gift, Affection's holiest token,
  The severed tress, which lay upon thy heart—
                    Canst thou forget?

Canst thou forget, belov'd one—comes there never
  The angel of sweet visions to thy rest?
Brings she not back the fond hopes fled for ever,
  While one lost name thrills through thy sleeping breast?—
                    Canst thou forget?

GRACE GREENWOOD.

65   9

MOONLIGHT NIGHT.

How beautiful this night ! The balmiest sigh
Which vernal zephyrs breathe in Evening's ear,
Were discord to the speaking quietude
That wraps this moveless scene. Heaven's ebon vault,
Studded with stars unutterably bright,
Through which the moon's unclouded grandeur rolls,
Seems like a canopy which Love had spread
To curtain her sleeping world. Yon gentle hills,
Robed in a garment of untrodden snow ;
Yon darksome walls, whence icicles depend
So stainless, that their white and glittering spears
Tinge not the moon's pure beam ; yon castled steep,
Whose banner hangeth o'er the time-worn tower
So idly, that wrapt Fancy deemeth it
A metaphor of Peace,—all form a scene
Where musing Solitude might love to lift
Her soul above this sphere of earthliness ;
Where Silence undisturb'd might watch alone,
So cold, so bright, so still.

SHELLEY.

66

GREEN leaves were here;
But 't was the foliage of the rocks—the birch,
The yew, the holly, and the bright green thorn,
With hanging islands of resplendent furze:
And on a summit, distant a short space,
By any who should look beyond the dell,
A single mountain cottage might be seen.

WORDSWORTH.

THEIR groves o' sweet myrtle let foreign lands reckon,
  Where bright beaming summers exalt the perfume ;
Far dearer to me yon lone glen o' green bracken,
  Wi' the burn stealing under the lang yellow broom.
Far dearer to me yon humble broom bowers,
Where the bluebell and gowan lurk lowly unseen.

BURNS.

COME awa', come awa',
 An' leave your Southland hame, lassie,
The kirk is near, the ring is here—
 An' I'm your Donald Græme, lassie:
Rock and reel, and spinning-wheel,
 And English cottage trig, lassie,
Haste, leave them a', wi' me to speel
 The braes 'yont Stirling brig, lassie.

PRINGLE.

TWILIGHT.

Hail Twilight, sovereign of one peaceful hour
Not dull art thou as undiscerning Night;
But studious only to remove from sight
Day's mutable distinctions.   Ancient power!
Thus did the waters gleam, the mountains lower
To the rude Briton, when, in wolf-skin vest
Here roving wild, he laid him down to rest
On the bare rock, or through a leafy bower
Looked ere his eyes were closed.   By him was seen
The selfsame vision which we now behold,
At thy meek bidding, shadowy power, brought forth;
These mighty barriers, and the gulf between;
The floods,—the stars; a spectacle as old
As the beginning of the heavens and earth.

WORDSWORTH.

O'ER the heath the heifer strays,
　　Free, the furrow'd task is done,
Now the village windows blaze,
　　Burnish'd by the setting sun.

Trudging as the ploughmen go,
　　To the smoking hamlet bound,
Giant-like their shadows grow,
　　Lengthened o'er the level ground.

———

THE slanting ray,
From every herb and every spiry blade,
Stretches a length of shadow o'er the field.
Mine, spindling into longitude immense,
In spite of gravity and sage remark
That I myself am but a fleeting shade,
Provokes me to a smile.

COWPER.

WEARIE'S WELL.

In a saft simmer gloamin',
  In yon dowie dell,
It was there we twa first met,
  By Wearie's cauld well.
We sat on the broom bank,
  And look'd in the burn,
But sidelang we look'd on
  Ilk ither in turn.

The corncraik was chirming
  His sad eerie cry,
And the wee stars were dreaming
  Their path through the sky;
The burn babbled freely
  Its love to ilk flower,
But we heard and we saw nought
  In that blessed hour.

We heard and we saw nought,
  Above or around;
We felt that our luve lived,
  And loathed idle sound.
I gazed on your sweet face
  Till tears fill'd my e'e,
And they drapt on your wee loof—
  A warld's wealth to me.

Now the winter snaw's fa'ing
  On bare holm and lea,
And the cauld wind is strippin'
  Ilk leaf aff the tree.
But the snaw fa's not faster,
  Nor leaf disna part
Sae sune frae the bough, as
  Faith fades in your heart.

You've waled out anither
  Your bridegroom to be;
But can his heart luve sae
  As mine luvit thee?
Ye'll get biggings and mailins,
  And mony braw claes;
But they a' winna buy back
  The peace o' past days.

Farewell, and for ever,
  My first luve and last;
May thy joys be to come—
  Mine live in the past.
In sorrow and sadness
  This hour fa's on me;
But light, as thy luve, may
  It fleet over thee!

MOTHERWELL.

SPRING.

Look all around thee ! How the Spring advances !
  New life is playing through the gay green trees ;
See how, in yonder bower, the light leaf dances
  To the bird's tread, and to the quivering breeze !
How every blossom in the sunlight glances !
  The winter frost to his dark cavern flees,
And earth, warm-waken'd, feels through every vein
The kindly influence of the vernal rain.
Now silvery streamlets, from the mountains stealing,
  Dance joyously the verdant vales along ;
Cold fear no more the songster's voice is sealing ;
  Down in the thick dark grove is heard his song ;
And, all their bright and lovely hues revealing,
  A thousand plants the field and forest throng ;
Light comes upon the earth in radiant showers,
And mingling rainbows play among the flowers.

Tieck.

THE WAYSIDE SPRING.

FAIR dweller by the dusty way,
  Bright saint within a mossy shrine,
The tribute of a heart to-day,
  Weary and worn, is thine.

The earliest blossoms of the year,
  The sweetbrier and the violet,
The pious hand of Spring has here
  Upon thy altar set.

And not alone to thee is given
  The homage of the pilgrim's knee;
But oft the sweetest birds of heaven
  Glide down and sing to thee.

Here daily from his beechen cell,
  The hermit squirrel steals to drink;
And flocks which cluster to their bell,
  Recline along thy brink.

And here the wagoner blocks his wheels,
  To quaff the cool and generous boon;
Here from the sultry harvest-fields
  The reapers rest at noon.

And oft the beggar mask'd with tan,
  In rusty garments grey with dust,
Here sits and dips his little can,
  And breaks his scanty crust;

And, lull'd beside thy whispering stream,
  Oft drops to slumber unawares,
And sees the angel of his dream
  Upon celestial stairs.

Dear dweller by the dusty way,
  Thou saint within a mossy shrine,
The tribute of a heart to-day,
  Weary and worn, is thine!

                              READ.

82

In November days,
When vapours rolling down the valleys made
A lonely scene more lonesome ; among woods
At noon ; and 'mid the calm of summer nights,
When, by the margin of the trembling lake,
Beneath the gloomy hills, I homeward went
In solitude, such intercourse was mine :
'T was mine among the fields both day and night,
And by the waters all the summer long.

WORDSWORTH.

For him the Spring
Distils her dew, and from the silken gem
Its lucid leaves unfolds; for him the hand
Of Autumn tinges every fertile branch
With blooming gold, and blushes like the morn.
Each passing hour sheds tribute from her wing;
And still new beauties meet his lonely walk,
And loves unfelt attract him. Not a breeze
Flies o'er the meadow, not a cloud imbibes
The setting sun's effulgence, not a strain
From all the tenants of the warbling shade
Ascends, but whence his bosom can partake
Fresh pleasure unreproved.

AKENSIDE.

CUSHLO-MO-CHREE.*

By the green banks of Shannon, I wooed thee, dear Mary,
  When the sweet birds were singing in summer's gay pride;
From those green banks I turn now, heart-broken and dreary,
  As the sun sets, to weep o'er the grave of my bride.
While the sweet birds around me are singing,
  Summer like winter is cheerless to me;
I heed not if snow falls, or flow'rets are springing,
  For my heart's light is darkened—my *Cushlo-mo-chree!*

Oh! bright shone the morning when first as my bride, love,
  Thy foot like a sunbeam my threshold cross'd o'er;
And blest on our hearth fell that soft eventide, love,
  When first on my bosom thy heart lay, *Asthore!*
Restlessly now, on my lone pillow turning,
  Wear the night-watches, still thinking on thee,
And darker than night breaks the light of the morning,
  For my aching eyes find thee not, *Cushlo-mo-chree!*

Oh, my loved one! my lost one! say, why didst thou leave me
  To linger on earth with my heart in the grave?
Oh, would thy cold arms, love, might ope to receive me
  To my rest 'neath the dark boughs that over thee wave!
Still from our once happy dwelling I roam, love,
  Evermore seeking, my own bride, for thee;
Oh, Mary! wherever thou art is my home, love,
  And I'll soon lie beside thee, my *Cushlo-mo-chree!*

JOHN FRANCIS WALLER, LL.D.

* "*Cushlo-mo-chree*"—Pulse of my heart.

MICHAEL.

UPON the forest-side in Grasmere Vale
There dwelt a Shepherd, Michael was his name;
An old man, stout of heart, and strong of limb.
His bodily frame had been, from youth to age,
Of an unusual strength; his mind was keen,
Intense, and frugal, apt for all affairs,
And in his shepherd's calling he was prompt
And watchful more than ordinary men.
So lived he till his eightieth year was past.
His days had not been past in singleness:

His Helpmate was a comely matron, old—
Though younger than himself full twenty years.
She was a woman of a stirring life,
Whose heart was in her house. . . . . . .
The Pair had but one inmate in their house,
An only child who had been born to them
When Michael, telling o'er his years, began
To deem that he was old,—in shepherd's phrase,
With one foot in the grave. This only son,´
With two brave sheep-dogs tried in many a storm,
The one of an inestimable worth,
Made all their household. . . . .

Down from the ceiling, by the chimney's edge,
Which in our ancient uncouth country style
Did with a huge projection overbrow
Large space beneath, as duly as the light
Of day grew dim, the Housewife hung a lamp.
There by the light of this old lamp they sat,
Father and son, while late into the night
The Housewife plied her own peculiar work.
This light was famous in its neighbourhood,
. . . . For, as it chanced,
Their cottage on a plot of rising ground
Stood single, with large prospect, north and south,
And from this constant light, so regular
And so far seen, the house itself, by all
Who dwelt within the limits of the Vale,
Both old and young, was named the Evening Star.

The Shepherd, if he loved himself, must needs
Have loved his Helpmate; but to Michael's heart
This son of his old age was yet more dear—
. . . . To the thoughts
Of the old man his only son was now
The dearest object that he knew on earth.
Exceeding was the love he bare to him.

And when by Heaven's good grace the boy grew up
A healthy lad, and carried in his cheek
Two steady roses that were five years old,
Then Michael from a winter coppice cut
With his own hand a sapling, which he hooped
With iron, making it throughout in all
Due requisites a perfect shepherd's staff,
And gave it to the boy; wherewith equipped
He as a watchman oftentimes was placed
At gate or gap, to stem or turn the flock;
And, to his office prematurely called,

There stood the urchin, as you will divine,
Something between a hindrance and a help;
Though nought was left undone which staff, or voice,
Or looks, or threatening gestures, could perform.

While in this sort the simple household lived
From day to day, to Michael's ear there came
Distressful tidings. Long before the time
Of which I speak, the Shepherd had been bound
In surety for his brother's son, .   .   .
.   .   .   .   And old Michael now
Was summoned to discharge the forfeiture,
A grievous penalty, but little less
Than half his substance. .   .   .   .   .   .

It seemed that his sole refuge was to sell
A portion of his patrimonial fields.
Such was his first resolve; he thought again,
And his heart failed him. "Isabel," said he,
Two evenings after he had heard the news,
"I have been toiling more than seventy years,
And in the open sunshine of God's love
Have we all lived; yet if these fields of ours
Should pass into a stranger's hand, I think
That I could not lie quiet in my grave.
Our Luke shall leave us, Isabel: the land
Shall not go from us, and it shall be free.
. . . . We have, thou know'st,
Another kinsman—he will be our friend
In this distress. He is a prosperous man,
Thriving in trade—and Luke to him shall go,
And with his kinsman's help and his own thrift
He quickly will repair this loss, and then
May come again to us." . . . . . .
. . . . At this the old man paused,
And Isabel sat silent. . . . .
These thoughts, and many others of like sort,
Passed quickly through the mind of Isabel,
And her face brightened. The old man was glad,
And thus resumed: . . . .
"Make ready Luke's best garments, of the best
Buy for him more, and let us send him forth
To-morrow, or the next day, or to-night:
If he could go, the boy should go to-night."
Here Michael ceased, and to the fields went forth
With a light heart. The Housewife for five days
Was restless morn and night, and all day long
Wrought on with her best fingers to prepare
Things needful for the journey of her son.
. . . . At length
The expected letter from their kinsman came,
With kind assurances that he would do

His utmost for the welfare of the boy;
To which requests were added that forthwith
He might be sent to him. . . . .

With morrow's dawn the boy
Began his journey, and when he had reached
The public way, he put on a bold face;
And all the neighbours, as he passed their doors,
Came forth with wishes and with farewell prayers,
That followed him till he was out of sight.
A good report did from their kinsman come,
Of Luke and his well-doing: and the boy
Wrote loving letters, full of wondrous news.
Both parents read them with rejoicing hearts.
So many months passed on. . . . . . .
. . . . Meantime Luke began
To slacken in his duty; and at length
He in his dissolute city gave himself
To evil courses: ignominy and shame

Fell on him, so that he was driven at last
To seek a hiding-place beyond the seas.

    I have conversed with more than one who well
Remembered the old man, and what he was
Years after he had heard this heavy news.
. . . . Among the rocks
He went, ...
And to that hollow dell from time to time
Did he repair to build the Fold of which
His Flock had need. . . . .
There by the Sheepfold, sometimes was he seen
Sitting alone, with that his faithful dog,
Then old, beside him, lying at his feet.
The length of full seven years, from time to time,
He at the building of this Sheepfold wrought,
And left the work unfinished when he died.
Three years, or little more, did Isabel
Survive her husband: at her death the estate
Was sold, and went into a stranger's hand.

WORDSWORTH.

LOVE.

WE met in secret, in the depth of night
When there was none to watch us; not an eye
Save the lone dweller of the lonely sky
To gaze upon our love and pure delight;
And in that hour's unbroken solitude,
When the white moon had robed her in its beam,
I've thought some vision of a blessed dream,
Or spirit of the air before me stood,
And held communion with me.   In mine ear
Her voice's sweet notes breathed not of the earth,
Her beauty seemed not of a mortal birth;
And in my heart there was an awful fear,
A thrill, like some deep warning from above,
That soothed its passion to a spirit's love.

FITZADAM.

'T is the merry nightingale
That crowds, and hurries, and precipitates
With thick fast warble his delicious notes,
As he were fearful that an April night
Would be too short for him to utter forth
His love-chant, and disburden his full soul
Of all its music.

COLERIDGE

SWEET bird, that sing'st away the early hours
Of winters past, or coming, void of care,
Well pleased with delights which present are,
Fair seasons, budding sprays, sweet-smelling flowers;
To rocks, to springs, to rills, from leafy bowers
Thou thy Creator's goodness dost declare,
And what dear gifts on thee He did not spare,
A stain to human sense in sin that lowers.
What soul can be so sick which by thy songs
(Attir'd in sweetness) sweetly is not driven
Quite to forget earth's turmoils, spites, and wrongs,
And lift a reverend eye and thought to Heaven?
Sweet artless songster, thou my mind dost raise
To airs of spheres, yes, and to angels' lays.

DRUMMOND.

13—2 **754686 A**

MINE be a cot beside the hill;
  A bee-hive's hum shall soothe my ear;
A willowy brook, that turns a mill,
  With many a fall, shall linger near.

The swallow oft, beneath my thatch,
  Shall twitter near her clay-built nest;
Oft shall the pilgrim lift the latch,
  And share my meal, a welcome guest.

Around my ivied porch shall spring
  Each fragrant flower that drinks the dew;
And Lucy, at her wheel, shall sing,
  In russet gown and apron blue.

The village church beneath the trees,
  Where first our marriage-vows were given,
With merry peals shall swell the breeze,
  And point with taper spire to heaven.

ROGERS.

Triumphal arch that fill'st the sky,
  When storms prepare to part,
I ask not proud philosophy
  To teach me what thou art.

Still seem, as to my childhood's sight,
  A mid-way station given
For happy spirits to alight,
  Betwixt the earth and heaven.

Can all that optics teach, unfold
  Thy form to please me so,
As when I dreamed of gems and gold
  Hid in thy radiant brow?

How glorious is thy girdle cast
  O'er mountain, tower, and town,
Or mirrored in the ocean vast,
  A thousand fathoms down!

For, faithful to its sacred page,
  Heaven still rebuilds thy span,
Nor lets the type grow pale with age
  That first spoke peace to man.

CAMPBELL.

Now who is he that bounds with joy
On Carrock's side, a shepherd boy?
No thoughts hath he but thoughts that pass
Light as the wind along the grass.
Can this be he who hither came
In secret, like a smothered flame?
O'er whom such thankful tears were shed
For shelter, and a poor man's bread!
God loves the Child ; and God hath willed
That those dear words should be fulfilled,
The Lady's words, when forced away,
The last she to her Babe did say :
"My own, my own, thy fellow-guest
I may not be ; but rest thee, rest,
For lowly shepherd's life is best!"

WORDSWORTH.

LONG TIME AGO.

NEAR the lake where drooped the willow,
  Long time ago!
Where the rock threw back the billow,
  Brighter than the snow;
Dwelt a maid beloved and cherished
  By high and low;
But with autumn's leaf she perished,
  Long time ago!

Rock, and tree, and flowing water,
  Long time ago!
Bird, and bee, and blossom taught her
  Love's spell to know!
While to my fond words she listened,
  Murmuring low,
Tenderly her dove-eyes glistened,
  Long time ago!

Mingled were our hearts for ever,
  Long time ago!
Can I now forget her? Never!
  No, lost one, no!
To her grave these tears are given,
  Ever to flow;
She's the star I missed from heaven,
  Long time ago!

G. P. MORRIS.

GLIDE gently, thus for ever glide,
  O Thames! that other bards may see
As lovely visions by thy side
  As now, fair river! come to me.
O glide, fair stream! for ever so,
  Thy quiet soul on all bestowing,
Till all our minds for ever flow
  As thy deep waters now are flowing.

Vain thought!—Yet be as now thou art,
  That in thy waters may be seen
The image of a poet's heart,
  How bright, how solemn, how serene!
Such as did once the Poet bless,
  Who, murmuring here a later ditty,
Could find no refuge from distress
  But in the milder grief of pity.

Now let us, as we float along,
  For *him* suspend the dashing oar;
And pray that never child of song
  May know that Poet's sorrows more.
How calm! how still! the only sound,
  The dripping of the oar suspended!
—The evening darkness gathers round
  By virtue's holiest powers attended.

WORDSWORTH.

A WINTER STORM.

On the passive main
Descends the eternal force, and with strong gust
Turns from its bottom the discolour'd deep.
Through the black night that sits immense around,
Lash'd into foam, the fierce conflicting brine
Seems o'er a thousand raging waves to burn.
Meantime the mountain-billows to the clouds
In dreadful tumult swell'd, surge above surge,
Burst into chaos with tremendous roar,
And anchor'd navies from their stations drive,
Wild as the winds across the howling waste
Of mighty waters : now the inflated wave
Straining they scale, and now impetuous shoot
Into the secret chambers of the deep.
Emerging thence again, before the breath
Of full-exerted heaven, they wing their course.

THOMSON.

110

HOCK-CART, OR HARVEST HOME.

COME, sons of summer, by whose toil
We are the lords of wine and oil;
By whose tough labours, and tough hands,
We rip up first, then reap our lands!
Crown'd with the ears of corn, now come,
And to the pipe sing "Harvest home."
Come forth, my lord, and see the cart
Drest up with all the country art.
See, here a manikin, there's a sheet
As spotless pure as it is sweet;
The horses, mares, and frisking fillies,
Clad all in linen white as lilies.
The harvest swains and wenches bound
For joy, to see the hock-cart crown'd.
About the cart hear how the rout
Of rural younglings raise the shout,
Pressing before, some coming after,—
Those with a shout, and these with laughter.
Some bless the cart, some kiss the sheaves,
Some prank them up with oaken leaves;
Some cross the thill-horse, some with great
Devotion stroke the home-borne wheat!
While other rustics, less attent
To prayers than to merriment,
Run after, with their garments rent.
Well on, brave boys! to your lord's hearth
Glittering with fire; where, for your mirth,
Ye shall see first the large and chief
Foundation of your feast—fat beef,

With upper stories—mutton, veal,
And bacon—which makes full the meal;
With several dishes standing by—
As here a custard, there a pie,
And here all-tempting frumenty.
And for to make the merry cheer,
If smirking wine be wanting here,
There's that which drowns all care—stout
    beer;
Which freely drink to your lord's health,
Then to the plough, the commonwealth;
Next to your flails, your fanes, your fats;
Then to the maids with wheaten hats.
To the rough sickle and crook'd scythe,
Drink, frolic boys, till all be blithe.
Feed and grow fat; and as ye eat,
Be mindful that the labouring neat,
As you, may have their full of meat;
And know besides, ye must revoke
The patient ox unto the yoke,
And all go back unto the plough
And harrow, though they're hang'd up now.
And you must know your lord's words
    true—
Feed him ye must whose food fills you;
And that this pleasure is like rain,
Not sent ye for to drown your pain,
But for to make it spring again.

HERRICK.

112

THERE was a Boy: ye knew him well, ye cliffs
And islands of Winander!—many a time,
At evening, when the earliest stars began
To move along the edges of the hills,
Rising or setting, would he stand alone,
Beneath the trees, or by the glimmering lake ;
And there, with fingers interwove, both hands
Pressed closely palm to palm and to his mouth
Uplifted, he, as through an instrument,
Blew mimic hootings to the silent owls,
That they might answer him.   And they would shout
Across the watery vale, and shout again,
Responsive to his call,—with quivering peals,
And long halloos, and screams, and echoes loud
Redoubled and redoubled ; concourse wild
Of mirth and jocund din ! And, when it chanced
That pauses of deep silence mocked his skill,
Then, sometimes, in that silence, while he hung
Listening, a gentle shock of mild surprise
Has carried far into his heart the voice
Of mountain-torrents ; or the visible scene
Would enter unawares into his mind
With all its solemn imagery, its rocks,
Its woods, and that uncertain heaven received
Into the bosom of the steady lake.

WORDSWORTH.

THE gleaners spread around, and here and there,
Spike after spike, their sparing harvest pick.
Be not too narrow, husbandmen ; but fling
From the full sheaf, with charitable stealth,
The liberal handful. Think, O grateful think,
How good the God of Harvest is to you,
Who pours abundance o'er your flowing fields!
While these unhappy partners of your kind
Wide hover round you, like the fowls of heaven,
And ask their humble dole.

THOMSON.

TO THE CUCKOO.

O BLITHE New-comer! I have heard,
I hear thee and rejoice;
O Cuckoo! shall I call thee bird,
Or but a wandering voice?

While I am lying on the grass,
Thy loud note smites my ear!
From hill to hill it seems to pass,
At once far off and near!

I hear thee babbling to the vale
Of sunshine and of flowers;
And unto me thou bring'st a tale
Of visionary hours.

Thrice welcome, darling of the Spring!
Even yet thou art to me
No bird, but an invisible thing,
A voice, a mystery;

The same who in my schoolboy days
I listened to; that cry
Which made me look a thousand ways
In bush, and tree, and sky.

To seek thee did I often rove
Through woods and on the green;
And thou wert still a hope, a love;
Still longed for, never seen!

And I can listen to thee yet;
Can lie upon the plain
And listen, till I do beget
That golden time again.

O blessed Bird! the earth we pace
Again appears to be
An unsubstantial, fairy place;
That is fit home for thee!

WORDSWORTH.

118

It is not only in the sacred fane
That homage should be paid to the Most High;
There is a temple, one not made with hands—
The vaulted firmament: Far in the woods,
Almost beyond the sound of city chime,
At intervals heard through the breezeless air;
When not the limberest leaf is seen to move,
Save where the linnet lights upon the spray;
When not a floweret bends its little stalk,
Save where the bee alights upon the bloom;
There, rapt in gratitude, in joy, and love,
The man of God will pass the Sabbath noon;
Silence his praise.

GRAHAME.

RUTH.

BENEATH her father's roof, alone
She seemed-to live; her thoughts her own;
  Herself her own delight:
Pleased with herself, nor sad, nor gay,
She passed her time; and in this way
  Grew up to woman's height.

There came a youth from Georgia's shore
A military casque he wore,
  With splendid feathers drest;
He brought them from the Cherokees;
The feathers nodded in the breeze,
  And made a gallant crest.

Among the Indians he had fought,
And with him many tales he brought
  Of pleasure and of fear;
Such tales as told to any maid
By such a Youth, in the green shade,
  Were perilous to hear.

And then he said, "How sweet it were
A fisher or a hunter there,
  A gardener in the shade,
Still wandering with an easy mind,
To build a household fire, and find
  A home in every glade!

"Sweet Ruth! and could you go with me
  My helpmate in the woods to be,
    Our shed at night to rear;
  Or run, my own adopted bride,
  A sylvan huntress at my side,
    And drive the flying deer!

"Beloved Ruth!"   No more he said.
Sweet Ruth alone at midnight shed
  A solitary tear:
She thought again—and did agree
With him to sail across the sea,
  And drive the flying deer.

"And now, as fitting is and right,
  We in the Church our faith will plight,
    A husband and a wife."
  Even so they did; and I may say
  That to sweet Ruth that happy day
    Was more than human life.

But now the pleasant dream was gone !
No hope, no wish remained, not one,—
　　They stirred him now no more ;
New objects did new pleasure give,
And once again he wished to live
　　As lawless as before.

Meanwhile, as thus with him it fared,
They for the voyage were prepared,
　　And went to the sea-shore ;
But, when they thither came, the Youth
Deserted his poor Bride, and Ruth
　　Could never find him more.

God help thee, Ruth !—Such pains she had
That she in half a year was mad,
　　And in a prison housed ;
And there, exulting in her wrongs,
Among the music of her songs,
　　She fearfully caroused.

When Ruth three seasons thus had lain,
There came a respite to her pain ;
　　She from her prison fled ;
But of the Vagrant none took thought ;
And where it liked her best she sought
　　Her shelter and her bread.

Among the fields she breathed again :
The master current of her brain
　　Ran permanent and free ;
And coming to the Banks of Tone,
There did she rest ; and dwell alone
　　Under the greenwood tree.

A barn her winter bed supplies;
But, till the warmth of summer skies
   And summer days is gone,
(And all do in this tale agree,)
She sleeps beneath the greenwood tree,
   And other home hath none.

WORDSWORTH.

NUNS fret not at their convent's narrow room;
And hermits are contented with their cells;
And students with their pensive citadels.
Maids at the wheel, the weaver at his loom,
Sit blithe and happy; bees that soar for bloom,
High as the highest Peak of Furness-Fells,
Will murmur by the hour in foxglove bells:
In truth, the prison unto which we doom
Ourselves, no prison is: and hence to me,
In sundry moods, 'twas pastime to be bound
Within the Sonnet's scanty plot of ground:
Pleased if some souls (for such there needs must be)
Who have felt the weight of too much liberty,
Should find short solace there, as I have found.

WORDSWORTH

TRUE LOVE.

TRUE love is but a humble, low-born thing,
And hath its food served up in earthen ware ;
It is a thing to walk with, hand in hand,
Through the every-dayness of this work-day world,
Baring its tender feet to every roughness,
Yet letting not one heart-beat go astray
From Beauty's law of plainness and content ;
A simple, fire-side thing, whose quiet smile
Can warm earth's poorest hovel to a home ;
Which, when our autumn cometh, as it must,
And life in the chill wind shivers bare and leafless,
Shall still be blest with Indian-summer youth
In bleak November, and, with thankful heart,
Smile on its ample stores of garnered fruit,
As full of sunshine to our aged eyes
As when it nursed the blossoms of our spring.
Such is true love, which steals into the heart,
With feet as silent as the lightsome dawn
That kisses smooth the rough brows of the dark,
And hath its will through blissful gentleness,—
Not like a rocket, which, with savage glare,
Whirrs suddenly up, then bursts, and leaves the night
Painfully quivering on the dazed eyes ;
A love that gives and takes, that seeth faults,
Not with flaw-seeking eyes like needle points,
But, loving kindly, ever looks them down
With the o'ercoming faith of meek forgiveness :
A love that shall be new and fresh each hour
As is the golden mystery of sunset,
Or the sweet coming of the evening star.
Alike, and yet most unlike, every day,
And seeming ever best and fairest now ;
A love that doth not kneel for what it seeks,
But faces Truth and Beauty as their peer,
Showing its worthiness of noble thoughts
By a clear sense of inward nobleness ;
A love that in its object findeth not
All grace and beauty, and enough to sate
Its thirst of blessing, but, in all of good
Found there, it sees but heaven-granted types
Of good and beauty in the soul of man ;
And traces in the simplest heart that beats,
A family-likeness to its chosen one,
That claims of it the rights of brotherhood.
For love is blind but with the fleshly eye,
That so its inner sight may be more clear ;
And outward shows of beauty only so
Are needful at the first, as is a hand

To guide and to uphold an infant's steps:
Great spirits need them not: their earnest look
Pierces the body's mask of thin disguise,
And beauty ever is to them revealed,
Behind the unshapeliest, meanest lump of clay,
With arms outstretched and eager face ablaze,
Yearning to be but understood and loved.

J. R. LOWELL.

THE REVERIE OF POOR SUSAN.

AT the corner of Wood Street, when daylight appears,
There's a Thrush that sings loud—it has sung for three years :
Poor Susan has passed by the spot, and has heard
In the silence of morning the song of the bird.

'T is a note of enchantment ; what ails her ? she sees
A mountain ascending, a vision of trees ;
Bright volumes of vapour through Lothbury glide,
And a river flows on through the vale of Cheapside.

Green pastures she views in the midst of the dale,
Down which she so often has tripped with her pail ;
And a single small cottage, a nest like a dove's,
The one only dwelling on earth that she loves.

She looks, and her heart is in heaven ; but they fade,
The mist and the river, the hill and the shade :
The stream will not flow, and the hill will not rise,
And the colours have all passed away from her eyes.

WORDSWORTH.

THE PLEASURES OF RETIREMENT.

THE man, who, from the world escaped,
In still retreats and flow'ry solitudes,
To Nature's voice attends, from month to month,
And day to day, through the revolving year;
Admiring, sees her in her ev'ry shape,
Feels all her sweet emotions at his heart;
Takes what she lib'ral gives, nor thinks of more.
He, when young Spring protrudes the bursting gems,
Marks the first bud, and sucks the healthful gale
Into his freshen'd soul; her genial hours
He full enjoys; and not a beauty blows,
And not an op'ning blossom breathes, in vain.

THOMSON.

133

THE BANKS OF THE WYE.

·FIVE years have pass'd; five summers, with the length
Of five long winters! and again I hear
These waters, rolling from their mountain springs
With a sweet inland murmur. Once again
Do I behold these steep and lofty cliffs,
Which on a wild secluded scene impress
Thoughts of more deep seclusion. . . . .
. . . . Though absent long,
These forms of beauty have not been to me
As is a landscape to a blind man's eye;
But oft in lonely rooms, and 'mid the din
Of towns and cities, I have owed to them,
In hours of weariness sensations sweet.
. . . . When the fretful stir
Unprofitable, and the fever of the world,
Have hung upon the beatings of my heart—
How oft, in spirit, have I turned to thee,
O sylvan Wye! . . . .
. . . . For I have learned
To look on Nature, not as in the hour
Of thoughtless youth. . . . .
. . . . And I have felt
A presence that disturbs me with the joy
Of elevated thoughts; a sense sublime
Of something far more deeply interfused,
Whose dwelling is the light of setting suns,
And the round ocean and the living air,
And the blue sky, and in the mind of man:
A motion and a spirit, that impels
All thinking things, all objects of all thought,
And rolls through all things. . . . .
. . Thou art with me here upon the banks
Of this fair river; thou, my dearest Friend,
My dear, dear Friend, and in thy voice I catch
The language of my former heart, and read
My former pleasures in the shooting lights

Of thy wild eyes. Oh! yet a little while
May I behold in thee what I was once,
My dear, dear Sister! . . . .
. . . . Therefore let the moon
Shine on thee in thy solitary walk;
And let the misty mountain winds be free
To blow against thee: and, in after years, . . .
If solitude, or fear, or pain, or grief,
Should be thy portion, with what healing thoughts

Of tender joy wilt thou remember me,
And these my exhortations! nor, perchance,
If I should be where I no more can hear
Thy voice, nor catch from thy wild eyes these gleams
Of past existence, wilt thou then forget
That on the banks of this delightful stream
We stood together. . . . .
. . . . Nor wilt thou then forget,
That after many wanderings, many years
Of absence, these steep woods and lofty cliffs,
And this green pastoral landscape, were to me
More dear, both for themselves and for thy sake!

WORDSWORTH.

A CALM.

WITH easy course
The vessels glide, unless their speed be stopped
By dead calms, that oft lie on those smooth seas,
While every zephyr sleeps;
    Then the shrouds drop,
The downy feather on the cordage hung
Moves not; the flat sea shines like yellow gold
Fused in the fire, or like the marble floor
Of some old temple wide; but where so wide,
In old or later time, its marble floor
Did ever temple boast as this, which here
Spreads its bright level many a league around?

DYER.

To YONDER hill, whose sides, deform'd and steep,
Just yield a scanty sust'nance to the sheep,
With thee, my friend, I oftentimes have sped,
To see the sun rise from his healthy bed;
To watch the aspect of the summer morn,
Smiling upon the golden fields of corn,
And taste, delighted, of superior joys,
Beheld through sympathy's enchanted eyes:
With silent admiration oft we view'd
The myriad hues o'er heaven's blue concave strew'd;
The fleecy clouds, of every tint and shade,
Round which the silvery sunbeam glancing play'd,
And the round orb itself, in azure throne,
Just peeping o'er the blue hill's ridgy zone:
We mark'd, delighted, how, with aspect gay,
Reviving nature hail'd returning day;
Mark'd how the flow'rets rear'd their drooping heads,
And the wild lambkins bounded o'er the meads,
While from each tree, in tones of sweet delight,
The birds sing pæans to the source of light:
Oft have we watch'd the speckled lark arise,
Leave his grass bed, and soar to kindred skies,
And rise, and rise, till the pain'd sight no more
Could trace him in his high aërial tour;
Though on the ear, at intervals, his song
Came wafted slow the wavy breeze along.

HENRY KIRKE WHITE.

And O ye Fountains, Meadows, Hills, and Groves,
Think not of any severing of our loves!
Yet in my heart of hearts I feel your might;
I only have relinquished one delight
To live beneath your more habitual sway.
I love the Brooks which down their channels fret,
Even more than when I tripped lightly as they:
The innocent brightness of a new-born Day
        Is lovely yet;
The clouds that gather round the setting sun
Do take a sober colouring from an eye
That hath kept watch o'er man's mortality;
Another race hath been and other palms are won.
Thanks to the human heart by which we live;
Thanks to its tenderness, its joys, and fears;
To me the meanest flower that blows can give
Thoughts that do often lie too deep for tears.

WORDSWORTH.

YARROW VISITED.

SEPTEMBER, 1814.

AND is this—Yarrow?—*This* the Stream
  Of which my fancy cherished,
So faithfully, a waking dream?
  An image that hath perished!
O that some Minstrel's harp were near,
  To utter notes of gladness,
And chase this silence from the air,
  That fills my heart with sadness!

Yet why?—a silvery current flows
  With uncontrolled meanderings;
Nor have these eyes by greener hills
  Been soothed, in all my wanderings.
And, through her depths, Saint Mary's Lake
  Is visibly delighted;
For not a feature of those hills
  Is in the mirror slighted.

A blue sky bends o'er Yarrow Vale,
  Save where that pearly whiteness
Is round the rising sun diffused,
  A tender hazy brightness;
Mild dawn of promise! that excludes
  All profitless dejection;
Though not unwilling here t' admit
  A pensive recollection.

Where was it that the famous Flower
  Of Yarrow Vale lay bleeding?
His bed perchance was yon smooth mound
  On which the herd is feeding:
And haply from this crystal pool,
  Now peaceful as the morning,
The Water-wraith ascended thrice,
  And gave his doleful warning.

Delicious is the Lay that sings
  The haunts of happy lovers,

The path that leads them to the grove,
  The leafy grove that covers:
And pity sanctifies the verse
  That paints, by strength of sorrow
The unconquerable strength of love
  Bear witness, rueful Yarrow!

But thou, that didst appear so fair
  To fond imagination,
Dost rival in the light of day
  Her delicate creation:
Meek loveliness is round thee spread,
  A softness still and holy;
The grace of forest charms decayed,
  And pastoral melancholy.

That region left, the Vale unfolds
  Rich groves of lofty stature,
With Yarrow winding through the pomp
  Of cultivated nature;
And, rising from those lofty groves,
  Behold a Ruin hoary!
The shattered front of Newark's Towers,
  Renowned in Border story.

Fair scenes for childhood's opening bloom,
  For sportive youth to stray in;
For manhood to enjoy his strength;
  And age to wear away in!
Yon cottage seems a bower of bliss;
  It promises protection
To studious ease, and generous cares,
  And every chaste affection!

How sweet, on this autumnal day,
  The wild-wood's fruits to gather,
And on my true-love's forehead plant
  A crest of blooming heather!

And what if I enwreathed my own !
  'T were no offence to reason ;
The sober hills thus deck their brows
  To meet the wintry season.

I see—but not by sight alone,
  Loved Yarrow, have I won thee :
A ray of fancy still survives—
  Her sunshine plays upon thee !
Thy ever-youthful waters keep
  A course of lively pleasure ;

And gladsome notes my lips can breathe,
  Accordant to the measure.

The vapours linger round the Heights,
  They melt—and soon must vanish ;
One hour is theirs, no more is mine—
  Sad thought ! which I would banish,
But that I know, where'er I go,
  Thy genuine image, Yarrow !
Will dwell with me—to heighten joy,
  And cheer my mind in sorrow.

WORDSWORTH.

MAIRE BHAN ASTÒR.[*]

In a valley far away,
  With my *Maire bhan Astòr*,
Short would be the summer day,
  Ever loving more and more.
Winter days would all grow long,
  With the light her heart would pour,
With her kisses and her song,
  And her loving *mait go lèor*.
    Fond is *Maire bhan Astòr*,
    Fair is *Maire bhan Astòr*,
    Sweet as ripple on the shore
    Sings my *Maire bhan Astòr*.

Oh! her sire is very proud,
  And her mother cold as stone;
But her brother bravely vowed
  She should be my bride alone;
For he knew I loved her well,
  And he knew she loved me too,
So he thought their pride to quell,
  But 't was all in vain to sue.
    True is *Maire bhan Astòr*,
    Tried is *Maire bhan Astòr*;
    Had I wings, I 'd never soar
    From my *Maire bhan Astòr*.

There are lands where manly toil
  Surely reaps the crop it sows;
Glorious wood and teeming soil,
  Where the broad Missouri flows;
Through the trees the smoke shall rise
  From our hearth with *mait go lèor*,
There shall shine the happy eyes
  Of my *Maire bhan Astòr*.
    Mild is *Maire bhan Astòr*,
    Mine is *Maire bhan Astòr*,
    Saints will watch about the door
    Of my *Maire bhan Astòr*.

                                   THOMAS DAVIS.

[*] *Maire bhan Astòr*—"Mary my treasure."

YE blessèd Creatures, I have heard the call
     Ye to each other make ; I see
The heavens laugh with you in your jubilee ;
     My heart is at your festival,
     My head hath its coronal,
The fulness of your bliss, I feel—I feel it all.
     Oh, evil day ! if I were sullen
     While the Earth herself is adorning,
          This sweet May morning ;
     And children are pulling
          On every side,
     In a thousand valleys far and wide,
     Fresh flowers ; while the sun shines **warm,**
And the Babe leaps up on his Mother's arm :—
     I hear, I hear, with joy I hear !
     — But there 's a Tree, of many, one,
A single Field which I have looked upon,
Both of them speak of something that is gone :
          The Pansy at my feet
          Doth the same tale repeat :
Whither is fled the visionary gleam ?
Where is it now, the glory and the dream ?

WORDSWORTH.

A CALM EVENING.

It is a beauteous Evening, calm and free :
The holy time is quiet as a Nun
Breathless with adoration ; the broad sun
Is sinking down in its tranquillity ;
The gentleness of heaven is on the sea :
Listen ! the mighty Being is awake,
And doth with his eternal motion make
A sound like thunder—everlastingly.
Dear Child ! dear Girl ! that walkest with me here,
If thou appear'st untouched by solemn thought,
Thy nature therefore is not less divine :
Thou liest "in Abraham's bosom" all the year ;
And worshipp'st at the Temple's inner shrine,
God being with thee when we know it not.

WORDSWORTH.

Now swarms the village o'er the jovial mead:
The rustic youth, brown with meridian toil,
Healthful and strong; full as the summer rose
Blown by prevailing suns, the ruddy maid,
Her kindled graces burning o'er her cheek.
E'en stooping age is here; and infant hands
Trail the long rake, or, with the fragrant load
O'ercharg'd, amid the kind oppression roll.
Wide flies the tedded * grain; all in a row
Advancing broad or wheeling round the field,
They spread the breathing harvest to the sun,
That throws refreshful round a rural smell;
Or, as they rake the green-appearing ground,
And drive the dusky wave along the mead,
The russet haycock rises thick behind,
In order gay; while heard from dale to dale,
Waking the breeze, resounds the blended voice
Of happy labour, love, and social glee.

THOMSON.

* *Tedded*, tossed, or spread about in the sun ; *to tede grass.*

THE OLD CUMBERLAND BEGGAR.

I saw an aged Beggar in my walk;
And he was seated by the highway side,
On a low structure of rude masonry
Built at the foot of a huge hill, that they
Who lead their horses down the steep rough road
May thence remount at ease. The aged man
Had placed his staff across the broad smooth stone
That overlays the pile; and, from a bag
All white with flour, the dole of village dames,
He drew his scraps and fragments, one by one,
And scanned them with a fixed and serious look
Of idle computation. In the sun,
Upon the second step of that small pile,
Surrounded by those wild unpeopled hills,
He sat, and ate his food in solitude:
And ever, scattered from his palsied hand,
That, still attempting to prevent the waste,
Was baffled still, the crumbs in little showers
Fell on the ground; and the small mountain birds,
Not venturing yet to pick their destined meal,
Approached within the length of half his staff.
Him from my childhood have I known; and then
He was so old, he seems not older now.
He travels on, a solitary man,—
His age has no companion. . . . .
. . . . Thus, from day to day,
Bow-bent, his eyes for ever on the ground,
He plies his weary journey. . . . . .
. . . . Poor Traveller!
His staff trails with him; scarcely do his feet
Disturb the summer dust; he is so still
In look and motion, that the cottage curs,
Ere he have passed the door, will turn away,
Weary of barking at him. Boys and girls,
The vacant and the busy, maids and youths,
And urchins newly breeched—all pass him by:
Him even the slow-paced waggon leaves behind.

But deem not this man useless. .   .   .   .   .   .
.   .   .   .   While thus he creeps
From door to door, the villagers in him
Behold a record which together binds
Past deeds and offices ot charity.
Among the farms and solitary huts,
Hamlets, and thinly scattered villages,
Where'er the aged Beggar takes his rounds,
The mild necessity of use compels
To acts of love ; and habit does the work
Of reason ; yet prepares that after-joy
Which reason cherishes. And thus the soul,

By that sweet taste of pleasure unpursued,
Doth find itself insensibly disposed
To virtue and true goodness.   .   .   .   .
.   .   .   .   All behold in him
A silent monitor.   .   .   .   .

My neighbour, when with punctual care, each week
Duly as Friday comes, though pressed herself
By her own wants, she from her chest of meal
Takes one unsparing handful for the scrip
Of this old Mendicant, and, from her door
Returning with exhilarated heart,
Sits by her fire, and builds her hope in Heaven.
Then let him pass, a blessing on his head!
And while in that vast solitude to which
The tide of things has led him, he appears
To breathe and live but for himself alone—
Unblamed, uninjured, let him bear about
The good which the benignant law of Heaven

Has hung around him; and, while life is his,
Still let him prompt the unlettered villagers
To tender offices and pensive thoughts.
Then let him pass, a blessing on his head!
And long as he can wander, let him breathe
The freshness of the valleys: let his blood
Struggle with frosty air and winter snows:
And let the chartered wind that sweeps the heath
Beat his grey locks against his withered face.
Be his the natural silence of old age!
Let him be free of mountain solitudes:
And have around him, whether heard or not,
The pleasant melody of woodland birds.
And let him, *where* and *when* he will, sit down
Beneath the trees, or by the grassy bank
Of highway side, and with the little birds
Share his chance-gathered meal; and, finally,
As in the eye of Nature he has lived,
So in the eye of Nature let him die!

WORDSWORTH.

A MOUNTAIN DWELLING.

You behold,

High on the breast of yon dark mountain, dark
With stony barrenness, a shining speck
Bright as a sunbeam sleeping, till a shower
Brush it away, or cloud pass over it ;
And such it might be deemed—a sleeping sunbeam ;
But 't is a plot of cultivated ground,
Cut off an island in the dusky waste ;
And that attractive brightness is its own.
The lofty site, by nature framed, to tempt,
Amid a wilderness of rocks and stones,
The tiller's hand, a hermit might have chosen,
For opportunity presented thence
Far forth to send his wandering eye o'er land
And ocean, and look down upon the works,
The habitations, and the ways of men,
Himself unseen. But no tradition tells
That ever hermit dipped his maple dish
In the sweet spring that lurks 'mid yon green fields,
And no such visionary views belong
To those who occupy and till the ground,
And on the bosom of the mountain dwell—
A wedded pair in childless solitude.
A house of stones collected on the spot,
By rude hands built, with rocky knolls in front,
Backed also by a ledge of rock, whose crest
Of birch-trees waves above the chimney-top ;
In shape, in size, and colour, an abode
Such as in unsafe times of border war
Might have been wished for and contrived, to elude
The eye of roving plunderer.

WORDSWORTH

THE WONDERS OF THE LANE.

STRONG climber of the mountain-side,
  Though thou the vale disdain,
Yet walk with me where hawthorns hide
  The wonders of the lane.
High o'er the rushy springs ot Don
  The stormy gloom is roll'd;
The moorland hath not yet put on
  His purple, green, and gold.
But here the titling * spreads his wing,
  Where dewy daisies gleam;
And here the sunflower † of the Spring
  Burns bright in morning's beam.
Oh, then, while hums the earliest bee,
  Where verdure fires the plain,
Walk thou with me, and stoop to see
  The glories of the lane!

ELLIOTT.

* The Hedge Sparrow.   † The Dandelion.

NUTTING.

                    IT seems a day
(I speak of one from many singled out),
One of those heavenly days which cannot die ;
When forth I sallied from our cottage-door,
With a huge wallet o'er my shoulder slung,
A nutting-crook in hand ; and turned my steps
Towards the distant woods, a Figure quaint,
Tricked out in proud disguise of cast-off weeds
Which for that service had been husbanded
By exhortation of my frugal Dame.
Motley accoutrement—of power to smile
At thorns, and brakes, and brambles,—and, in truth,
More ragged than need was ! Among the woods,
And o'er the pathless rocks, I forced my way,
Until at length I came to one dear nook
Unvisited, where not a broken bough
Drooped with its withered leaves, ungracious sign
Of devastation ; but the hazels rose
Tall and erect, with milk-white clusters hung,
A virgin scene ! A little while I stood,
Breathing with such suppression of the heart
As joy delights in ; and, with wise restraint
Voluptuous, fearless of a rival, eyed
The banquet ; or beneath the trees I sat
Among the flowers, and with the flowers I played ;
A temper known to those, who, after long
And weary expectation, have been blessed
With sudden happiness beyond all hope.
Perhaps it was a bower beneath whose leaves
The violets of five seasons reappear
And fade, unseen by any human eye ;
Where fairy water-breaks do murmur on
For ever ; and I saw the sparkling foam,
And—with my cheek on one of those green stones
That, fleeced with moss, beneath the shady trees,
Lay round me, scattered like a flock of sheep—
I heard the murmur and the murmuring sound,
In that sweet mood when pleasure loves to pay
Tribute to ease ; and, of its joy secure,
The heart luxuriates with indifferent things,
Wasting its kindliness on stocks and stones,
And on the vacant air. Then up I rose,
And dragged to earth both branch and bough, with crash
And merciless ravage ; and the shady nook,
Of hazels, and the green and mossy bower,
Deformed and sullied, patiently gave up
Their quiet being : and, unless I now
Confound my present feelings with the past,

Even then, when from the bower I turned away
Exulting, rich beyond the wealth of kings,
I felt a sense of pain when I beheld
The silent trees and the intruding sky.
Then, dearest Maiden, move along these shades
In gentleness of heart ; with gentle hand
Touch—for there is a spirit in the woods.

WORDSWORTH.

THAT cottage, with its walls so white, and gabled roof so quaint;
Oh! was it not a chosen thing for artist hands to paint?
With casement windows, where the vine festoon'd the angled panes;
And trellised porch, where woodbine wove its aromatic chains.
Ah! Memory yet keeps the spot with fond and holy care;
I know the shape of every branch that flung its shadow there;
And 'mid the varied homes I 've had—oh! tell me which has vied
With that of merry Childhood by the Green Hill-side?

ELIZA COOK.

THE TWO APRIL MORNINGS.

WE walked along, while bright and red
  Uprose the morning sun ;
And Matthew stopped, he looked, and said,
  "The will of God be done!"

A village schoolmaster was he,
  With hair of glittering gray ;
As blithe a man as you could see
  On a Spring holiday.

And on that morning, through the grass,
  And by the streaming rills,
We travelled merrily, to pass
  A day among the hills.

"Our work," said I, "was well begun ;
  Then from thy breast what thought,
Beneath so beautiful a sun,
  So sad a sigh has brought?"

A second time did Matthew stop ;
  And fixing still his eye
Upon the eastern mountain-top,
  To me he made reply :

"Yon cloud with that long purple cleft
  Brings fresh into my mind
A day like this, which I have left
  Full thirty years behind.

"And just above yon slope of corn
  Such colours, and no other,
Were in the sky that April morn,
  Of this the very brother.

THE TWO APRIL MORNINGS.

"With rod and line I sued the sport
    Which that sweet season gave,
And, coming to the church, stopped short
    Beside my daughter's grave.

"Nine summers had she scarcely seen,
    The pride of all the vale;
And then she sang;—she would have been
    A very nightingale!

"Six feet in earth my Emma lay;
    And yet I loved her more,
For so it seemed, than till that day
    I e'er had loved before.

"And, turning from her grave, I met,
    Beside the churchyard yew,
A blooming Girl, whose hair was wet
    With points of morning dew.

"A basket on her head she bare;
    Her brow was smooth and white;
To see a child so very fair,
    It was a pure delight!

"No fountain from its rocky cave
    E'er tripped with foot so free;
She seemed as happy as a wave
    That dances on the sea.

"There came from me a sigh of pain
    Which I could ill confine;
I looked at her, and looked again:
    —And did not wish her mine."

THE TWO APRIL MORNINGS.

Matthew is in his grave; yet now,
  Methinks, I see him stand,
As at that moment, with his bough
  Of wilding in his hand.

WORDSWORTH.

HENCE good and evil mixed, but man has skill
And power to part them, when he feels the will !
Toil, care, and patience bless th' abstemious few,
Fear, shame, and want the thoughtless herd pursue.

Behold the Cot ! where thrives th' industrious swain,
Source of his pride, his pleasure, and his gain ;
Screen'd from the winter's wind, the sun's last ray
Smiles on the window and prolongs the day
Projecting thatch the woodbine's branches stop,
And turn their blossoms to the casement's top :
All need requires is in that cot contain'd,
And much that taste untaught and unrestrain'd
Surveys delighted.

CRABBE.

It is the hour when from the boughs
  The nightingale's high note is heard ;
It is the hour when lovers' vows
  Seem sweet in every whisper'd word ;
And gentle winds, and waters near,
Make music to the lonely ear.
Each flower the dews have lightly wet,
And in the sky the stars are met,
And on the wave is deeper blue,
And on the leaf a browner hue,
·And in the heaven that clear obscure,
So softly dark, and darkly pure,
Which follows the decline of day,
As twilight melts beneath the moon away.

BYRON.

THE MOTHER'S SONG.

Her eyes are wild, her head is bare,
The sun has burnt her coal-black hair;
Her eyebrows have a rusty stain,
And she came far from o'er the main.
  She has a Baby on her arm,
    Or else she were alone;
  And underneath the haystack warm,
    And on the greenwood stone,
She talked and sung the woods among,
And it was in the English tongue.

"Sweet Babe! they say that I am mad,
  But nay, my heart is far too glad;
  And I am happy when I sing
  Full many a sad and doleful thing;
    Then, lovely Baby, do not fear!
      I pray thee have no fear of me,
    But, safe as in a cradle here,
      My lovely Baby! thou shalt be:
To thee I know too much I owe;
I cannot work thee any woe.

"A fire was once within my brain;
  And in my head a dull, dull pain;
  And fiendish faces, one, two, three,
  Hung at my breasts, and pulled at me.
    But then there came a sight of joy;
      It came at once to do me good;
    I waked, and saw my little Boy,
      My little Boy of flesh and blood;
Oh joy for me that sight to see!
For he was here, and only he.

"Oh! love me, love me, little Boy!
  Thou art thy mother's only joy;
  And do not dread the waves below,
  When o'er the sea-rock's edge we go;
    The high crag cannot work me harm,
      Nor leaping torrents when they howl;
    The Babe I carry on my arm,
      He saves for me my precious soul:
Then happy lie; for blessed am I;
Without me my sweet Babe would die.

"Then do not fear, my Boy! for thee
  Bold as a lion I will be;
  And I will always be thy guide
  Through hollow snows and rivers wide.
    I'll build an Indian bower; I know
      The leaves that make the softest bed;
    And, if from me thou wilt not go,
      But still be true till I am dead,
My pretty thing! then thou shalt sing
As merry as the birds in Spring.

"Oh! smile on me, my little Lamb!
  For I thy own dear mother am.
  My love for thee has well been tried:
  I've sought thy father far and wide.
    I know the poisons of the shade,
      I know the earth-nuts fit for food;
    Then, pretty dear, be not afraid;
      We'll find thy father in the wood.
Now laugh and be gay, to the woods away!
And there, my Babe, we'll live for aye."

WORDSWORTH.

Ask not the boy, who, when the breeze ol morn
First shakes the glitt'ring drops from ev'ry thorn,
Unfolds his flock, then under bank or bush
Sits linking cherry-stones, or platting rush,
How fair is freedom? He was always free.
To carve his rustic name upon a tree,
To snare the mole, or with ill-fashioned hook
To draw th' incautious minnow from the brook,
Are life's prime pleasures in his simple view,
His flock the chief concern he ever knew:
She shines but little in his heedless eyes;
The good we never miss, we rarely prize.

COWPER.

175

THREE YEARS SHE GREW IN SUN AND SHOWER.

THREE years she grew in sun and shower,
Then Nature said, "A lovelier flower
  On earth was never sown;
This child I to myself will take,
She shall be mine, and I will make
  A lady of my own.

"Myself will to my darling be
Both law and impulse, and with me
  The girl in rock and plain,
In earth and heaven, in glade and bower,
Shall feel an overseeing power
  To kindle or restrain.

"She shall be sportive as the fawn,
That wild with glee across the lawn
  Or up the mountain springs;
And hers shall be the breathing palm,
And hers the silence and the calm
  Of mute insensate things.

"The floating clouds their state shall lend
To her—for her the willow bend;
  Nor shall she fail to see
Even in the motions of the storm,
Grace that shall mould the maiden's form
  By silent sympathy.

"The stars of midnight shall be dear
To her, and she shall lean her ear
  In many a secret place;
Where rivulets dance their wayward round,
And beauty, born of murmuring sound,
  Shall pass into her face.

"And vital feelings of delight
   Shall rear her form to stately height ;
      Her virgin bosom swell.
Such thoughts to Lucy I will give,
While she and I together live
      Here in this happy dell."

Thus Nature spake—the work was done—
How soon my Lucy's race was run !
   She died, and left to me
This heath, this calm and quiet scene,
The memory of what has been,
      And never more will be.

WORDSWORTH.

PLEASING 't is, O modest moon !
Now the night is at her noon,
'Neath thy sway to musing lie,
While around the zephyrs sigh,
Fanning soft the sun-tann'd wheat,
Ripen'd by the summer's heat ;
Picturing all the rustic's joy
When boundless plenty greets his eye.

HENRY KIRKE WHITE.

23—2

THE FORCE OF PRAYER;

OR, THE FOUNDING OF BOLTON PRIORY.

A TRADITION.

" What is good for a bootless bene ? "
    With these dark words begins my tale ;
And their meaning is, " Whence can comfort spring,
    When prayer is of no avail ? "

" What is good for a bootless bene ? "
    The falconer to the Lady said ;
And she made answer, " ENDLESS SORROW ! "
    For she knew that her son was dead.

She knew it by the falconer's words,
    And from the look of the falconer's eye ;
And from the love which was in her soul
    For her youthful Romilly.

—Young Romilly through Barden Woods
    Is ranging high and low ;
And holds a greyhound in a leash,
    To let slip upon buck or doe.

And the pair have reached that fearful chasm,
    How tempting to bestride !
For lordly Wharf is there pent in
    With rocks on either side.

This striding-place is called THE STRID,
    A name which it took of yore :
A thousand years hath it borne that name,
    And shall a thousand more.

180

And hither is young Romilly come,
  And what may now forbid
That he, perhaps for the hundredth time,
  Shall bound across "The Strid"?

He sprang in glee,—for what cared he
  That the river was strong, and the rocks were steep
—But the greyhound in the leash hung back,
  And checked him in his leap.

The boy is in the arms of Wharf,
  And strangled by a merciless force ;
For never more was young Romilly seen
  Till he rose a lifeless corse.

Now there is stillness in the vale,
  And long unspeaking sorrow :
Wharf shall be to pitying hearts
  A name more sad than Yarrow.

If for a lover the Lady wept,
  A solace she might borrow
From death, and from the passion of death :
  Old Wharf might heal her sorrow.

She weeps not for the wedding-day
  Which was to be to-morrow :
Her hope was a farther-looking hope,
  And hers a mother's sorrow.

He was a tree that stood alone,
  And proudly did its branches wave ;
And the root of this delightful tree
  Was in her husband's grave !

THE FORCE OF PRAYER.

Long, long in darkness did she sit,
  And her first words were, "Let there be
In Bolton, on the field of Wharf,
  A stately Priory!"

The stately Priory was reared;
  And Wharf, as he moved along,
To Matins joined a mournful voice,
  Nor failed at Even-song.

And the Lady prayed in heaviness
  That looked not for relief!
But slowly did her succour come,
  And a patience to her grief.

Oh! there is never sorrow of heart
  That shall lack a timely end,
If but to God we turn, and ask
  Of Him to be our friend!

WORDSWORTH.

THE JOYS OF HOME.

SWEET are the joys of home,
  And pure as sweet; for they,
Like dews of morn and evening, come
  To wake and close the day.

The world hath its delights,
  And its delusions too;
But home to calmer bliss invites,
  More tranquil and more true.

The mountain flood is strong,
  But fearful in its pride;
While gently rolls the stream along
  The peaceful valley's side.

Life's charities, like light,
  Spread smilingly afar;
But stars approach'd become more bright,
  And home is life's own star.

The pilgrim's step in vain
  Seeks Eden's sacred ground!
But in home's holy joys, again
  An Eden may be found.

A glance of heaven to see,
  To none on earth is given;
And yet a happy family
  Is but an earlier heaven.

JOHN BOWRING.

Among those joys, 't is one at eve to sail
On the broad River with a favourite gale;
When no rough waves upon the bosom ride,
But the keel cuts, nor rises on the tide;
Safe from the stream the nearer gunwale stands,
Where playful children trail their idle hands:
Or strive to catch long grassy leaves that float
On either side of the impeded boat;
What time .the moon arising shows the mud,
A shining border to the silver flood.

Crabbe.

WHEN, in the south, the wan noon, brooding still,
Breathed a pale steam around the glaring hill,
And shades of deep-embattled clouds were seen,
Spotting the northern cliffs with lights between;
Gazing the tempting shades to them denied,
When stood the shortened herds amid the tide,
Where from the barren wall's unsheltered end
Long rails into the shallow lake extend.

WORDSWORTH.

I THINK OF THEE.

I THINK of thee—I think of thee,
And all that thou hast borne for me ;
In hours of gloom or heartless glee,
I think of thee—I think of thee !

When fiercest rage the storms of Fate,
And all around is desolate ;
I pour on life's tempestuous sea
The oil of peace—with thoughts of thee !

When Fortune frowns and hopes deceive
    me,
And summer friends in sorrow leave me ;
A Timon, from the world I flee—
My wreck of wealth—sweet dreams of
    thee !

Or if I join the careless crowd,
Where laughter peals and mirth grows
    loud,
Even in my hours of revelry,
I turn to thee—I turn to thee !

I think of thee—I think and sigh
O'er blighted years and bliss gone by ;
And mourn the stern, severe decree,
That spared me only thoughts of thee !

In Youth's gay spring, 'mid Pleasure's
    bowers,
Where all is sunshine, mirth, and flowers,
We met ;—I bent the adoring knee,
And told a tender tale to thee !

'T was summer's eve—the heavens above,
Earth—ocean—air—were full of love :
Nature around kept jubilee
When first I breathed that tale to thee !

The crystal clouds that hung on high
Were blue as thy delicious eye ;—
The stirless shore, and sleeping sea,
Seem'd emblems of repose and thee !

I spoke of hope—I spoke of fear ;—
Thy answer was a blush and tear :—
But this was eloquence to me,
And more than I had ask'd of thee !

I look'd into thy dewy eye,
And echoed thy half-stifled sigh ;
I clasp'd thy hand—and vow'd to be
The soul of love and truth to thee !

The scene and hour have pass'd—yet still
Remains a deep impassion'd thrill ;
A sunset glow on memory,
That kindles at each thought of thee !

We loved—how wildly and how well,
'T were worse than idle now to tell :
From love and life alike thou 'rt free,
And I am left to think of thee !

Though years—long years have darkly
    sped,
Since thou wert number'd with the dead,
In fancy oft thy form I see ;
In dreams, at least, I 'm still with thee !

Thy beauty, helplessness, and youth ;
Thy hapless fate, untiring truth ;
Are spells that often touch the key
Of sweet, harmonious thoughts of thee !

.

The bitter frown of friends estranged,
The chilling straits of fortunes changed ;

All this—and more—thou 'st borne for
  me—
Then how can I be false to thee ?

.

I never will :—I 'll think of thee
Till fades the power of memory ;
In weal or woe—in gloom or glee—
I 'll think of thee—I 'll think of thee !

ALARIC A. WATTS.

RESOLUTION AND INDEPENDENCE.

A GENTLE answer did the old man make,
  In courteous speech which forth he slowly drew;
And him with further words I thus bespake:
"What kind of work is that which you pursue?
  This is a lonesome place for one like you."
He answered me with pleasure and surprise,
And there was, while he spake, a fire about his eyes.

He told me that he to this pond had come
  To gather leeches, being old and poor:
Employment hazardous and wearisome!
  And he had many hardships to endure:
  From pond to pond he roamed, from moor to moor;
Housing, with God's good help, by choice or chance;
And in this way he gained an honest maintenance.

The old man still stood talking by my side;
  But now his voice to me was like a stream
Scarce heard; nor word from word could I divide;
  And the whole body of the man did seem
  Like one whom I had met with in a dream;
Or, like a man from some far region sent,
To give me human strength and strong admonishment.

WORDSWORTH.

My ramble ended, I returned ;
  Beau, trotting far before,
The floating wreath again discerned,
  And plunging, left the shore.

I saw him, with that lily cropped,
  Impatient swim to meet
My quick approach, and soon he dropped
  The treasure at my feet.

Charmed with the sight, the world, I cried,
  Shall hear of this thy deed :
My dog shall mortify the pride
  Of man's superior breed :

But chief myself I will enjoin,
  Awake at duty's call,
To show a love as prompt as thine
  To Him who gives me all.

COWPER.

THE BROOK.

BROOK! whose society the Poet seeks,
Intent his wasted spirits to renew;
And whom the curious Painter doth pursue
Through rocky passes, among flowery creeks,
And tracks thee dancing down thy water-breaks;
If I some type of thee did wish to view,
Thee, and not thee thyself, I would not do
Like Grecian Artists, give thee human cheeks,
Channels for tears; no Naiad shouldst thou be,
Have neither limbs, feet, feathers, joints, nor hairs.
It seems the Eternal Soul is clothed in thee
With purer robes than those of flesh and blood,
And hath bestowed on thee a better good—
Unwearied joy, and life without its cares.

WORDSWORTH

Nor yet less pleasing at the heavenly throne,
The Sabbath service of the shepherd boy!
In some lone glen, where every sound is lulled
To slumber, save the tinkling of the rill,
Or bleat of lamb, or hovering falcon's cry,
Stretched on the sward, he reads of Jesse's son;
Or sheds a tear o'er him to Egypt sold,
And wonders why he weeps; the volume closed,
With thyme-sprig laid between the leaves, he sings
The sacred lays, his weekly lesson, conned
With meikle care beneath the lowly roof,
Where humble lore is learnt, where humble worth
Pines unrewarded by a thankless state.
Thus reading, hymning, all alone, unseen,
The shepherd boy the Sabbath holy keeps,
Till on the heights he marks the straggling bands
Returning homeward from the house of prayer.

GRAHAME.

THE BLIND HIGHLAND BOY.

A TALE TOLD BY THE FIRESIDE.

He ne'er had seen one earthly sight ;
The sun, the day ; the stars, the night ;
Or tree, or butterfly, or flower,
Or fish in stream, or bird in bower,
    Or woman, man, or child.

Beside a lake their cottage stood,
Not small, like ours, a peaceful flood ;
But one of mighty size, and strange ;
That, rough or smooth, is full of change,
    And stirring in its bed.

But what do his desires avail?
For he must never handle sail,
Nor mount the mast, nor row, nor float
In sailor's ship or fisher's boat
    Upon the rocking waves.

THE BLIND HIGHLAND BOY.

When one day (now mark me well,
Ye soon shall know how this befell)
He's in a vessel of his own,
On the swift water hurrying down
    Towards the mighty sea.

But say what bears him? . . . . .
The shell of a green Turtle, thin
And hollow; you might sit therein,
    It was so wide and deep.

'T was even the largest of its kind,
Large, thin, and light as birch-tree rind,
So light a shell that it would swim,
And gaily lift its fearless brim
    Above the tossing surge.

And this the litttle blind Boy knew:
And he a story strange, yet true,
Had heard, how in a shell like this
An English boy, O thought of bliss!
    Had stoutly launched from shore.

A bold thought roused him, and he took
The shell from out its secret nook,
    And bore it in his arms.

And with the happy burthen hied,
And pushed it from Loch Leven's side,—
Stepped into it; and, without dread,
Following the fancies in his head,
    He paddled up and down.

Awhile he stood upon his feet;
He felt the motion—took his seat;
And dallied thus, till from the shore
The tide, retreating more and more,
    Had sucked, and sucked him in.

THE BLIND HIGHLAND BOY.

But when he was first seen, oh me,
What shrieking and what misery! . . .

And quickly, with a silent crew,
A boat is ready to pursue;
And from the shore their course they take,
And swiftly down the running lake
　　They follow the blind Boy.

And then, when he was brought to land,
Full sure they were a happy band,
Which, gathering round, did on the banks
Of that great water give God thanks,
　　And welcomed the poor Child.

WORDSWOR

Full six hundred years have fled,
  And the Abbey pile is scatter'd;
War and ruin have been spread,
  Blood been spilt, and keystones shatter'd.
Ivy-stalks are running over
  Cloister wall and oriel top;
Bluebell-cups and snowy clover
  Tempt the first young bees to stop.
High and wild the grass is growing,
  Where the altar shrine was raised;
There the fresh Spring wind is blowing,
  There the wandering kine have grazed.

ELIZA COOK.

For he was one in all their idle sport,
And like a monarch ruled their little court;
The pliant bow he form'd, the flying ball,
The bat, the wicket, were his labours all.

CRABBE.

I HAVE seen
A curious child, who dwelt upon a tract
Of inland ground, applying to his ear
The convolutions of a smooth-lipped shell;
To which, in silence hushed, his very soul
Listened intensely; and his countenance soon
Brightened with joy; for murmurings from within
Were heard,—sonorous cadences! whereby,
To his belief, the monitor expressed
Mysterious union with its native sea.
Even such a shell the universe itself
Is to the ear of faith; and there are times,
I doubt not, when to you it doth impart
Authentic tidings of invisible things;
Of ebb and flow, and ever-during power;
And central peace subsisting at the heart
Of endless agitation.   Here you stand,
Adore, and worship, when you know it not:
Pious beyond the intention of your thought,
Devout above the meaning of your will.
Yes, you have felt, and may not cease to feel.
The estate of man would be indeed forlorn,
If false conclusions of the reasoning power
Made the eye blind, and closed the passages
Through which the ear converses with·the heart.
Has not the soul, the being of your life,
Received a shock of awful consciousness,
In some calm season, when these lofty rocks
At night's approach bring down the unclouded sky
To rest upon their circumambient walls?
A temple framing of dimensions vast,
And yet not too enormous for the sound
Of human anthems,—choral song, or burst
Sublime of instrumental harmony,
To glorify the Eternal! What if these
Did never break the stillness that prevails
Here—if the solemn nightingale be mute,
And the soft woodlark here did never chant

ADVANCING Spring profusely spreads abroad
Flowers of all hues, with sweetest fragrance stored ;
Where'er she treads Love gladdens every plain,
Delight on tiptoe bears her lucid train ;
Sweet Hope with conscious brow before her flies,
Anticipating wealth from summer skies ;
All Nature feels her renovating sway,
The sheep-fed pasture and the meadow gay';
And trees and shrubs, no longer budding seen,
Display the new-grown branch of lighter green ;
On airy downs the idling shepherd lies,
And sees to-morrow in the marbled skies.

BLOOMFIELD.

Down the sultry arc of day,
The burning wheels have urged their way,
And eve along the western skies
Sheds her intermingling dyes.
Down the deep, the miry lane,
Creaking comes the empty wain,
And Driver on the shaft-horse sits,
Whistling now and then by fits ;
And oft, with his accustomed call,
Urging on the sluggish Ball.
The barn is still, the master's gone,
And Thresher puts his jacket on,
While Dick, upon the ladder tall,
Nails the dead kite to the wall.
Here comes Shepherd Jack at last,
He has penned the sheep-cote fast,
For 't was but two nights before,
A lamb was eaten on the moor,
His empty wallet Rover carries,
Nor for Jack, when near home, tarries.

HENRY KIRKE WHITE.

HAVING reached the house,
I found its rescued inmate safely lodged,
And in serene possession of himself,
Beside a genial fire that seemed to spread
A gleam of comfort o'er his pallid face.
Great show of joy the Housewife made, and truly
Was glad to find her conscience set at ease;
And not less glad, for sake of her good name,
That the poor sufferer had escaped with life.
But though at first he seemed to have received
No harm, and uncomplaining as before
Went through his usual tasks, a silent change
Soon showed itself: he lingered three short weeks;
And from the Cottage hath been borne to-day.

WORDSWORTH.

Mount slowly, sun! and may our journey lie
Awhile within the shadow of this hill,
This friendly hill, a shelter from thy beams!
Such is the summer pilgrim's frequent wish;
And as that wish, with prevalence of thanks
For present good o'er fear of future ill,
Stole in among the morning's blither thoughts,
'Twas chased away, for towards the western side
Of the broad vale, casting a casual glance,
We saw a throng of people; wherefore met?
Blithe notes of music, suddenly let loose
On the thrilled ear, did to the question yield
Prompt answer; they proclaim the annual Wake,
Which the bright season favours. Tabor and pipe
In purpose joined to hasten and reprove
The laggard Rustic; and repay with boons
Of merriment a parti-coloured knot,
Already formed upon the village green.
Beyond the limits of the shadow cast
By the broad hill, glistened upon our sight
That gay assemblage. Round them and above,
Glitter, with dark recesses interposed,
Casement, and cottage roof, and stems of trees
Half-veiled in vapoury cloud, the silver steam
Of dews fast melting on their leafy boughs
By the strong sunbeams smitten. Like a mast
Of gold, the Maypole shines; as if the rays
Of morning, aided by exhaling dew,
With gladsome influence could reanimate
The faded garlands dangling from its sides.

WORDSWORTH.

Sheep grazed the field ; some with soft bosom pressed
The herb as soft, while nibbling stray'd the rest ;
Nor noise was heard but of the hasty brook,
Struggling, detain'd in many a petty nook.
All seemed so peaceful, that, from them convey'd,
To me their peace by kind contagion spread.

Cowper.

So ABEL, pondering on his state forlorn,
Look'd round for comfort, and was chased by scorn.
And now we saw him on the beach reclined,
Or causeless walking in the wintry wind;
And when it raised a loud and angry sea,
He stood and gazed, in wretched reverie:
He heeded not the frost, the rain, the snow,
Close by the sea he walk'd alone and slow.

CRABBE.

ELLEN IRWIN;

OR, THE BRAES OF KIRTLE.

FAIR Ellen Irwin, when she sate
  Upon the Braes of Kirtle,
Was lovely as a Grecian maid
  Adorned with wreaths of myrtle.
Young Adam Bruce beside her lay ;
And there did they beguile the day
With love and gentle speeches,
Beneath the budding beeches.

From many Knights and many Squires
  The Bruce had been selected ;
And Gordon, fairest of them all,
  By Ellen was rejected.
Sad tidings to that noble youth !
For it may be proclaimed with truth,
If Bruce had loved sincerely,
That Gordon loves as dearly.

But what is Gordon's beauteous face,
  And what are Gordon's crosses,
To them who sit in Kirtle's Braes
  Upon the verdant mosses?
Alas that ever he was born !
The Gordon, couched behind a thorn,
Sees them and their caressing,
Beholds them blest and blessing.

Proud Gordon cannot bear the thoughts
  That through his brain are travelling,—
And, starting up, to Bruce's heart
  He launched a deadly javelin !

Fair Ellen saw it when it came,
And, stepping forth to meet the same,
Did with her body cover
The youth, her chosen lover.

And, falling into Bruce's arms,
  Thus died the beauteous Ellen,
Thus from the heart of her true love
  The mortal spear repelling.
And Bruce, as soon as he had slain
The Gordon, sailed away to Spain,
And fought with rage incessant
Against the Moorish Crescent.

But many days, and many months,
  And many years ensuing,
This wretched Knight did vainly seek
  The death that he was wooing ;
And, coming back across the wave,
Without a groan, on Ellen's grave
His body he extended,
And there his sorrow ended.

Now ye, who willingly have heard
  The tale I have been telling,
May in Kirkonnel churchyard view
  The grave of lovely Ellen :
By Ellen's side the Bruce is laid ;
And, for the stone upon his head,
May no rude hand deface it,
And its forlorn HIC JACET !

WORDSWORTH.

WATERS, bright Waters, how sweetly ye glide
Where the tapering bulrush stands up in your tide ;
Where the white lilies peep and the green cresses creep,
And your whimple just lulleth the minnow to sleep.
Now lurking in silence, all lonely you take
Your meandering course through the close-tangled brake ;
Where the adder may wink as he basks on the brink,
And the fox-cub and timid fawn fearlessly drink.
'Mid valley and greenwood right onward ye ramble,
Through the maze of the rushes and trail of the bramble ;
Where the Bard with his note, and the child with his boat,
Will linger beside ye to dream and to dote.
For a moment the mill-wheel may waken your wrath,
And disturb the repose of your silvery path ;
But your passionate spray falls like rainbows at play,
And as gently as ever ye steal on your way,
Humming a song as ye loiter along,
Looking up in the face of a shadowless day.
Waters, bright Waters, how sweetly ye glide
In the brooklet, with blossoms and birds by your side !

ELIZA COOK.

BUT trees, and rivulets whose rapid course
Defies the check of winter, haunts of deer,
And sheep-walks populous with bleating lambs,
And lanes, in which the primrose ere her time
Peeps through the moss that clothes the hawthorn root,
Deceive no student. Wisdom there, and truth,
Not shy as in the world, and to be won
By slow solicitation, seize at once
The roving thought, and fix it on themselves.

COWPER.

I LOVED the old man, for I pitied him.
A task it was, I own, to hold discourse
With one so slow in gathering up his thoughts,
But he was a cheap pleasure to my eyes;
Mild, inoffensive, ready in *his* way,
And useful to his utmost power: and there
Our Housewife knew full well what she possessed
He was her vassal of all labour, tilled
Her garden, from the pasture fetched her kine
And, one among the orderly array
Of haymakers, beneath the burning sun
Maintained his place; or heedfully pursued
His course, on errands bound to other vales,
Leading sometimes an inexperienced child,
Too young for any profitable task.
So moved he like a shadow that performed
Substantial service.

WORDSWORTH.

29—2

THE SOLITARY REAPER.

BEHOLD her, single in the field,
 Yon solitary Highland lass !
Reaping and singing by herself ;
 Stop here, or gently pass !
Alone she cuts and binds the grain,
And sings a melancholy strain.
Oh, listen ! for the Vale profound
Is overflowing with the sound.

No nightingale did ever chaunt
 So sweetly to reposing bands
Of travellers in some shady haunt,
 Among Arabian sands :
No sweeter voice was ever heard
In Spring-time from the cuckoo-bird,
Breaking the silence of the seas
Among the farthest Hebrides.

Will no one tell me what she sings ?
 Perhaps the plaintive numbers flow
For old, unhappy, far-off things,
 And battles long ago ;
Or is it some more humble lay,
Familiar matter of to-day ?
Some natural sorrow, loss, or pain,
That has been, and may be again !

Whate'er the theme the Maiden sang
 As if her song could have no ending,
I saw her singing at her work,
 And o'er the sickle bending ;—
I listened till I had my fill ;
And, as I mounted up the hill,
The music in my heart I bore,
Long after it was heard no more.

WORDSWORTH.

Rover, awake! the grey cock crows!
Come, shake your coat and go with me!
High in the east the green hill glows,
And glory crowns our shelt'ring tree.
The sheep expect us at the fold:
My faithful dog, let 's haste away,
And in his earliest beams behold,
And hail, the source of cheerful day.
Half his broad orb o'erlooks the hill,
And darting down the valley flies,
At every casement welcome still,
The golden summons of the skies.
Go, fetch my staff; and o'er the dews
Let echo waft thy gladsome voice.
Shall we a cheerful note refuse
When rising morn proclaims " Rejoice"?

BLOOMFIELD

231

THE IDLE SHEPHERD BOYS.

Again :—his heart within him dies—
His pulse is stopped, his breath is lost,
He totters, pale as any ghost,
And, looking down, he spies
A lamb, that in the pool is pent
Within that black and frightful rent.

The lamb had slipped into the stream,
And safe without a bruise or wound
The cataract had borne him down
Into the gulf profound.
His dam had seen him when he fell,
She saw him down the torrent borne :
And, while with all a mother's love
she from the lofty rocks above
Sent forth a cry forlorn.
The lamb, still swimming round and round,
Made answer to that plaintive sound.

When he had learnt what thing it was
That sent this rueful cry, I ween
The Boy recovered heart, and told
The sight which he had seen.
Both gladly now deferred their task :
Nor was there wanting other aid ;—
A Poet, one who loves the brooks
Far better than the sages' books,
By chance had hither stray'd ; . . . .
He drew it gently from the pool,
And brought it forth into the light :
The Shepherds met him with his charge,
An unexpected sight !
Into their arms the lamb they took,
Said they, " He's neither maimed nor scarred."
Then up the steep ascent they hied,
And placed him at his mother's side.

WORDSWORTH.

THE LITTLE WINTER GRAVE.

Our baby lies under the snow, sweet wife,
　Our baby lies under the snow,
Out in the dark with the night,
　While the winds so loudly blow.
As a dead saint thou art pale, sweet wife,
　And the cross is on thy breast;
Oh, the snow no more can chill
　That little dove in its nest!

Shall we shut the baby out, sweet wife,
　While the chilling winds do blow?
Oh, the grave is now its bed,
　And its coverlid is snow.
Oh, our merry bird is snared, sweet wife,
　That the rain of music gave,
And the snow falls on our hearts,
　And our hearts are each a grave.

Oh, it was the lamp of our life, sweet wife!
　Blown out in a night of gloom;
A leaf from our flower of love,
　Nipped in its fresh Spring bloom.
But the lamp will shine above, sweet wife,
　And the leaf again shall grow,
Where there are no bitter winds,
　And no dreary, dreary snow.

SHELDON CHADWICK.

SWEET Highland Girl, a very shower
Of beauty is thy earthly dower!
Twice seven consenting years have shed
Their utmost bounty on thy head:
And these grey rocks; this household lawn;
These trees, a veil just half withdrawn;
This fall of water, that doth make
A murmur near the silent lake;
This little bay; a quiet road
That holds in shelter thy abode;
In truth, together do ye seem
Like something fashioned in a dream;
Such forms as from their covert peep
When earthly cares are laid asleep!
Yet, dream and vision as thou art,
I bless thee with a human heart!
God shield thee to thy latest years!
I neither know thee nor thy peers,
And yet my eyes are filled with tears.

WORDSWORTH.

THE FOUNTAIN.

WE talked with open heart, and tongue
  Affectionate and true,
A pair of friends, though I was young,
  And Matthew seventy-two.

We lay beneath a spreading oak,
  Beside a mossy seat ;
And from the turf a fountain broke,
  And gurgled at our feet.

" Now, Matthew ! let us try to match
  This water's pleasant tune
With some old border song, or catch,
  That suits a summer's noon.

" Or of the church-clock and the chimes
  Sing here, beneath the shade,
That half-mad thing of witty rhymes
  Which you last April made !"

In silence Matthew lay, and eyed
  The spring beneath the tree ;
And thus the dear old man replied,
  The grey-haired man of glee :

" Down to the vale this water steers,
  How merrily it goes !
'T will murmur on a thousand years,
  And flow as now it flows.

" And here, on this delightful day
  I cannot choose but think
How oft, a vigorous man, I lay
  Beside this fountain's brink.

" My eyes are dim with childish tears,
  My heart is idly stirr'd,
For the same sound is in my ears
  Which in those days I heard.

" Thus fares it still in our decay :
  And yet the wiser mind
Mourns less for what age takes away
  Than what it leaves behind.

" The blackbird in the summer trees,
  The lark upon the hill,
Let loose their carols when they please,
  Are quiet when they will.

" With Nature never do *they* wage
  A foolish strife ; they see
A happy youth, and their old age
  Is beautiful and free :

" But we are pressed by heavy laws
  And often, glad no more,
We wear a face of joy, because
  We have been glad of yore.

" If there is one who need bemoan
  His kindred laid in earth,
The household hearts that were his own,
  It is the man of mirth.

" My days, my friend, are almost gone,
  My life has been approved,
And many love me ; but by none
  Am I enough beloved."

" Now both himself and me he wrongs,
  The man who thus complains !
I live and sing my idle songs
  Upon these happy plains ;

" And, Matthew, for thy children dead,
  I 'll be a son to thee !"
At this he grasped my hand, and said,
  " Alas ! that cannot be."

We rose up from the fountain-side ;
  And down the smooth descent
Of the green sheep-track did we glide ;
  And through the wood we went ;

And, ere we came to Leonard's Rock,
  He sang those witty rhymes
About the crazy old church-clock,
  And the bewildered chimes.

WORDSWORTH.

THE country was enclosed; a wide
And sandy road had banks on either side;
Where, lo! a hollow on the left appear'd,
And there a gipsy tribe their tent had rear'd;
'T was open spread, to catch the morning sun,
And they had now their early meal begun,
When two brown boys just left their grassy seat,
The early Trav'ller with their prayers to greet.
While yet Orlando held his pence in hand,
He saw their sister on her duty stand;
Some twelve years old, demure, affected, sly,
Prepared the force of early powers to try:
Sudden a look of langour he descries,
And well-feigned apprehension in her eyes;
Train'd but yet savage, in her speaking face
He mark'd the features of her vagrant race,
When a light laugh and roguish leer express'd
The vice implanted in her youthful breast.
Forth from the tent her elder brother came,
Who seem'd offended, yet forbore to blame
The young designer, but could only trace
The looks of pity in the Trav'ller's face.

CRABBE.

We rose up from the fountain-side ;
  And down the smooth descent
Of the green sheep-track did we glide ;
  And through the wood we went ;

And, ere we came to Leonard's Rock,
  He sang those witty rhymes
About the crazy old church-clock,
  And the bewildered chimes. .

WORDSWORTH.

THE country was enclosed; a wide
And sandy road had banks on either side;
Where, lo! a hollow on the left appear'd,
And there a gipsy tribe their tent had rear'd;
'T was open spread, to catch the morning sun,
And they had now their early meal begun,
When two brown boys just left their grassy seat,
The early Trav'ller with their prayers to greet.
While yet Orlando held his pence in hand,
He saw their sister on her duty stand;
Some twelve years old, demure, affected, sly,
Prepared the force of early powers to try:
Sudden a look of langour he descries,
And well-feigned apprehension in her eyes;
Train'd but yet savage, in her speaking face
He mark'd the features of her vagrant race,
When a light laugh and roguish leer express'd
The vice implanted in her youthful breast.
Forth from the tent her elder brother came,
Who seem'd offended, yet forbore to blame
The young designer, but could only trace
The looks of pity in the Trav'ller's face.

CRABBE.

O JOY! that in our embers
Is something that doth live,
That Nature yet remembers
What was so fugitive!
The thought of our past years in me doth breed
Perpetual benedictions: not indeed
For that which is most worthy to be blest;
Delight and liberty, the simple creed
Of Childhood, whether busy or at rest,
With new-fledg'd hope still fluttering in his breast:
Not for these I raise
The song of thanks and praise;
But for those obstinate questionings
Of sense and outward things,
Fallings from us, vanishings;
Blank misgivings of a Creature
Moving about in worlds not realized,
High instincts before which our mortal Nature
Did tremble, like a guilty thing surprised!
But for those first affections
Those shadowy recollections,
Which, be they what they may,
Are yet the fountain light of all our day,
Are yet a master light of all our seeing;
Uphold us—cherish—and have power to make
Our noisy years seem moments in the being
Of the eternal Silence: truths that wake,
To perish never;
Which neither listlessness, nor mad endeavour,
Nor Man nor Boy,
Nor all that is at enmity with joy,
Can utterly abolish or destroy!
Hence, in a season of calm weather,
Though inland far we be,
Our Souls have sight of that immortal Sea
Which brought us hither;
Can in a moment travel thither—
And see the Children sport upon the shore,
And hear the mighty waters rolling evermore.

WORDSWORTH.

Ocean exhibits, fathomless and broad,
Much of the power and majesty of God.
He swathes about the swelling of the deep,
That shines and rests, as infants smile and sleep.
Vast as it is, it answers as it flows
The breathings of the lightest air that blows;
Curling and whit'ning over all the waste,
The rising waves obey th' increasing blast,
Abrupt and horrid as the tempest roars,
Thunder and flash upon the steadfast shores,
Till He, that rides the whirlwind, checks the rein,
Then all the world of waters sleeps again.

COWPER.

GLEN ALMAIN; OR, THE NARROW GLEN.

In this still place, remote from men,
Sleeps Ossian, in the Narrow Glen;
In this still place, where murmurs on
But one meek streamlet, only one,
He sang of battles, and the breath
Of stormy war, and violent death;
And should, methinks, when all was past,
Have rightfully been laid at last
Where rocks were rudely heaped, and rent
As by a spirit turbulent;
Where sights were rough, and sounds were wild,
And everything unreconcil'd;
In some complaining dim retreat,
For fear and melancholy meet;
But this is calm: there cannot be
A more entire tranquillity.

Does then the Bard sleep here indeed?
Or is it but a groundless creed?
What matters it?—I blame them not
Whose fancy in this lonely spot
Was moved, and in this way express'd
Their notion of its perfect rest.
A convent, even a hermit's cell,
Would break the silence of this Dell:
It is not quiet, is not ease;
But something deeper far than these:
The separation that is here
Is of the grave; and of austere
And happy feelings of the dead:
And therefore was it rightly said
That Ossian, last of all his race!
Lies buried in this lonely place.

WORDSWORTH.

THE KITTEN AND THE FALLING LEAVES.

THAT way look, my Infant, lo
What a pretty baby-show!
See the Kitten on the wall,
Sporting with the leaves that fall,
Withered leaves—one—two—and three—
From the lofty elder tree!
Through the calm and frosty air
Of this morning bright and fair,
Eddying round and round they sink,
Softly, slowly: one might think,
From the motions that are made,
Every little leaf conveyed
Sylph or Fairy hither tending,—
To his lower world descending,
Each invisible and mute,
In this wavering parachute.
——But the Kitten, how she starts,
Crouches, stretches, paws, and darts!
First at one, and then its fellow,
Just as light and just as yellow;
There are many now—now one—
Now they stop, and there are none.
What intenseness of desire
In her upward eye of fire!
With a tiger-leap half-way
Now she meets the coming prey,
Lets it go as fast, and then
Has it in her power again:
Now she works with three or four,
Like an Indian conjuror;
Quick as he in feats of art,
Far beyond in joy of heart.
Were her antics played in the eye
Of a thousand standers-by,
Clapping hands with shout and stare,
What would little Tabby care

For the plaudits of the crowd?
Over happy to be proud,
Over wealthy in the treasure
Of her own exceeding pleasure!

*   *   *   *   *   *

And I will have my careless season,
Spite of melancholy reason :
Will walk through life in such a way
That, when time brings on decay,
Now and then I may possess
Hours of perfect gladsomeness.
—Pleased by any random toy ;
By a kitten's busy joy,
Or an infant's laughing eye
Sharing in the ecstacy.

WORDSWORTH.

THE MAYING.

FAIR May unveils her ruddy cheek,
And decks her brow with daisies,
And scatters blossoms as she goes
Through fields and forest mazes.
The fragrant hawthorn, white with bloom,
Fills all the uplands airy:
The grass is dry, the sky is clear—
Let's go a-Maying, Mary!

I dearly love, in days like this,
When birds make music o'er us,
To roam with thee through wildwood paths,
And listen to the chorus;
To help thee over crags and stiles,
And take thy hand in leaping,
And out and in to see thy face
Through leaves and branches peeping.

Ten years have pass'd since first I saw
Thy fresh and budding beauty;
And love has ripen'd with the years,
And link'd itself with duty.
In life's young Spring I swore to thee
A truth that should not vary;
And now, in summer of my days,
I love thee better, Mary!

Time lays his finger light on thee :
Thy cheeks are red as peaches ;
Thine eyes are bright as first they glow'd
To hear my youthful speeches.
Thine eldest boy is nine years old,
Thy youngest babe two summers ;
And thou art blooming like a girl,
'Mid all the little comers.

Bring all the four into the woods—
We'll set them gathering posies
Of harebells blue and pimpernels,
Instead of garden roses.
Beneath the trees we'll have one day
Of frolicsome employment ;
And birds shall sing and winds shall blow,
To help us to enjoyment.

Leave house affairs to shift awhile—
Leave work, and care, and sorrow ;
We'll be the merrier to-day,
And happier to-morrow.
I would not greatly care for life,
If Fate and Toil contrary
Could not afford me now and then
A holiday with Mary.

And Fate is kind to those who strive
To make existence pleasant,
With harmless joys and simple tastes,
And kindness ever present.
We'll not complain; so come away,
And when we want a treasure,
We'll use these May-day memories
To buy forgotten pleasure.

CHARLES MACKAY.

WEDDED LOVE.

This fair Bride—
In the devotedness of youthful love,
Preferring me to parents and the choir
Of gay companions, to the natal roof,
And all known places and familiar sights
(Resigned with sadness gently weighing down
Her trembling expectations, but no more
Than did to her due honour, and to me
Yielded, that day, a confidence sublime
In what I had to build upon)—this Bride,
Young, modest, meek, and beautiful, I led
To a low cottage in a sunny bay,
Where the salt sea innocuously breaks,
And the sea-breeze as innocently breathes,
On Devon's leafy shores; a sheltered hold,
In a soft clime encouraging the soil
To a luxuriant bounty! As our steps
Approach th' embowered abode—our chosen seat—
See, rooted in the earth, its kindly bed,
Th' unendangered myrtle, decked with flowers,
Before the threshold stands to welcome us!
While, in the flowering myrtle's neighbourhood,
Not overlooked, but courting no regard,
Those native plants, the holly and the yew,
Gave modest intimation to the mind
Of willingness with which they would unite
With the green myrtle, t' endear the hours
Of winter, and protect that pleasant place.
Wild were the walks upon those lonely Downs,
Track leading into track; how marked, how worn
Into bright verdure, among fern and gorse,
Winding away its never-ending line
On their smooth surface, evidence was none:
But, there, lay open to our daily haunt,
A range of unappropriated earth,
Where youth's ambitious feet might move at large;
Whence, unmolested wanderers, we beheld

The shining giver of the day diffuse
His brightness o'er a tract of sea and land
Gay as our spirits, free as our desires,
As our enjoyments boundless. From those heights
We dropped, at pleasure, into sylvan combs;
Where arbours of impenetrable shade,
And mossy seats, detained us side by side,
With hearts at ease, and knowledge in our hearts
"That all the grove and all the day was ours."

WORDSWORTH

Lo, YONDER shed! observe its garden ground,
With the low paling, form'd of wreck, around:
There dwells a fisher: if you view his boat,
With bed and barrel—'t is his house afloat;
Look at his house, where ropes, nets, blocks abound,
Tar, pitch, and oakum—'t is his boat aground:
That space enclosed but little he regards,
Spread o'er with relics of masts, sails, and yards;
Fish by the wall, on spit of elder, rest,
Of all his food the cheapest and the best,
By his own labour caught, for his own hunger dress'd.

Here our reformers come not; none object
To paths polluted, or upbraid neglect;
None care that ashy heaps at doors are cast,
That coal-dust flies along the blinding blast;
None heed the stagnant pools on either side,
Where new-launch'd ships of infant sailors ride:
Rodneys in rags here British valour boast,
And lisping Nelsons fright the Gallic coast;
They fix the rudder, set the swelling sail,
They point the bowsprit, and they blow the gale.

CRABBE.

How SWEET it is, when mother Fancy rocks
The wayward brain, to saunter through a wood!
An old place, full of many a lovely brood,
Tall trees, green arbours, and ground flowers in flocks;
And wild rose tip-toe upon hawthorn stocks,
Like to the bonny lass, who plays her pranks
At Wakes and Fairs with wandering Mountebanks,—
When she stands cresting the Clown's head, and mocks
The crowd beneath her. Verily I think,
Such place to me is sometimes like a dream
Or map of the whole world: thoughts, link by link,
Enter through ears and eyesight, with such gleam
Of all things, that at last in fear I shrink,
And leap at once from the delicious stream.

WORDSWORTH

33

THE GRAVES OF A HOUSEHOLD.

(See Frontispiece.)

THEY grew in beauty side by side,
   They filled one home with glee,
Their graves are severed far and wide,
   By mount, and stream, and sea.

The same fond mother bent at night
   O'er each fair sleeping brow,
She had each folded flower in sight—
   Where are those dreamers now?

One 'midst the forests of the West,
   By a dark stream is laid ;
The Indian knows his place of rest
   Far in the cedar shade.
The sea, the blue lone sea, hath one,
   He lies where pearls lie deep :
He was the loved of all, yet none
   O'er his low bed may weep.

One sleeps where southern vines are drest
   Above the noble slain ;
He wrapt his colours round his breast
   On a blood-red field of Spain.
And one—o'er her the myrtle showers
   Its leaves, by soft winds fanned ;
She faded 'midst Italian flowers,
   The last of that bright band.

And, parted thus, they rest—who played
   Beneath the same green tree,
Whose voices mingled as they prayed
   Around one parent knee :
They that with smiles lit up the hall,
   And cheered with song the hearth,—
Alas for love, if thou wert all,
   And nought beyond, O earth !

MRS. HEMANS.

SELECTIONS

FROM

BEATTIE'S "MINSTREL."

THE warbling woodland, the resounding shore,
The pomp of groves, and garniture of fields;
All that the genial ray of morning gilds.

AND lo,
The trees with foliage, cliffs with flowers are crowned ;
Pure rills through vales of verdure warbling go ;
And wonder, love, and joy, the peasant's heart o'erflow.

The waters, bursting from their slimy bed,
Bring health and melody to every vale :
And, from the breezy main, and mountain's head,
Ceres and Flora, to the sunny dale,
To fan their glowing charms, invite the fluttering gale.

With gold and gems if Chilian mountains glow ;
If bleak and barren Scotia's hills arise ;
There plague and poison, lust and rapine grow ;
Here peaceful are the vales, and pure the skies,
And Freedom fires the soul and sparkles in the eyes.

ALL that echoes to the song of even,
All that the mountain's sheltering bosom shields.

THE shepherd swain of whom I mention made,
On Scotia's mountains fed his little flock ;
The sickle, scythe, or plough he never swayed ;
An honest heart was almost all his stock ;
His drink, the living water from the rock :
The milky dams supplied his board, and lent
Their kindly fleece to baffle winter's shock ;
And he, though oft with dust and sweat besprent,
Did guide and guard their wanderings, wheresoe'er they went.

Rise, sons of harmony, and hail the morn,
While warbling larks on russet pinions float :
Or seek at noon the woodland scene remote,
Where the grey linnets carol from the hill.
Oh, let them ne'er, with artificial note,
To please a tyrant, strain the little bill,
But sing what Heaven inspires, and wander where they will.

WHEN o'er the sky advanced the kindling dawn,
The crimson cloud, blue main, and mountain grey,
And lake, dim-gleaming on the smoky lawn;
Far to the west, the long, long vale withdrawn,
Where twilight loves to linger for a while.

On his vows the blameless Phœbe smiled,
And her alone he loved, and loved her from a child.

No jealousy their dawn of love o'ercast,
Nor blasted were their wedded days with strife ;
Each season looked delightful as it passed,
To the fond husband and the faithful wife.

WHERE the maze of some bewildered stream
To deep untrodden groves his footsteps led ;
There would he wander wild, till Phœbus' beam,
Shot from the western cliff, released the weary team.

Lo ! WHERE the stripling, wrapt in wonder, roves
Beneath the precipice o'erhung with pine ;
And sees, on high, amidst th' encircling groves,
From cliff to cliff the foaming torrents shine :
While waters, woods, and winds in concert join,
And Echo swells the chorus to the skies.

In truth, he was a strange and wayward wight,
Fond of each gentle and each dreadful scene.
In darkness and in storm he found delight ;
Nor less, than when on ocean-wave serene
The southern sun diffused his dazzling sheen.
The raven croaks forlorn on naked spray ;
And, hark ! the river bursting every mound,
Down the vale thunders, and with wasteful sway
Uproots the grove, and rolls the shattered rocks away.

AND oft the craggy cliff he loved to climb,
When all in mist the world below was lost.
What dreadful pleasure! there to stand sublime,
Like shipwrecked mariner on desert coast,
And view th' enormous waste of vapour, tossed
In billows, lengthening to th' horizon round,
Now scooped in gulfs, with mountains now embossed!
And hear the voice of mirth and song rebound,
Flocks, herds, and waterfalls, along the hoar profound!

Is YONDER wave the sun's eternal bed?
Soon shall the Orient with new lustre burn,
And Spring shall soon her vital influence shed,
Again attune the grove, again adorn the mead.

SEE, in the rear of the warm sunny shower
The visionary boy from shelter fly ;
For now the storm of summer rain is o'er,
And cool, and fresh, and fragrant is the sky.
And, lo ! in the dark east, expanded high,
The rainbow brightens to the setting sun !
Fond fool, that deem'st the streaming glory nigh,
How vain the chase thine ardour has begun !
'T is fled afar, ere half thy purposed race be run.

WHEN the long-sounding curfew from afar
Loaded with loud lament the lonely gale,
Young Edwin, lighted by the evening star,
Lingering and listening, wandered down the vale.

Or, when the setting moon, in crimson dyed,
Hung o'er the dark and melancholy deep,
To haunted stream, remote from man, he hied,
Where Fays of yore their revels wont to keep;
And there let Fancy rove at large, till sleep
A vision brought to his entrancèd sight.

THE cottage curs at early pilgrim bark :
Crowned with her pail the tripping milkmaid sings ;
The whistling ploughman stalks afield ; and, hark !
Down the rough slope the ponderous waggon rings ;
Through rustling corn the hare astonished springs ;
Slow tolls the village clock the drowsy hour ;
The partridge bursts away on whirring wings ;
Deep mourns the turtle in sequestered bower,
And shrill lark carols clear from her aërial tower.

E'EN now his eyes with smiles of rapture glow,
As on he wanders through the scenes of morn,
Where the fresh flowers in living lustre blow,
Where thousand pearls the dewy lawns adorn,
A thousand notes of joy in every breeze are borne.

But who the melodies of morn can tell?
The wild brook babbling down the mountain-side ;
The lowing herd ; the sheepfold's simple bell ;
The pipe of early shepherd dim descried
In the lone valley ; echoing far and wide
The clamorous horn along the cliffs above ;
The hollow murmur of the ocean tide ;
The hum of bees, the linnet's lay of love,
And the full choir that wakes the universal grove.

SAVE when against the winter's drenching rain,
And driving snow, the cottage shut the door.

THEN, as instructed by tradition hoar,
Her legend when the Beldam 'gan impart,
Or chant the old heroic ditty o'er,
Wonder and joy ran thrilling to his heart;
Much he the tale admired, but more the tuneful art.

THENCE musing onward to the sounding shore,
The lone enthusiast oft would take his way,
Listening, with pleasing dread, to the deep roar
Of the wide-weltering waves.

In black array
When sulphurous clouds rolled on th' autumnal day;
E'en then he hastened from the haunt of man,
Along the trembling wilderness to stray,
What time the lightning's fierce career began,
And o'er heaven's rending arch the rattling thunder ran.

ONE cultivated spot there was, that spread
Its flowery bosom to the noonday beam,
Where many a rose-bud rears its blushing head,
And herbs for food with future plenty teem.
Soothed by the lulling sound of grove and stream,
Romantic visions swarm on Edwin's soul.

Art, empire, earth itself, to change are doomed ;
Earthquakes have raised to heaven the humble vale,
And gulfs the mountain's mighty mass entombed.

Now BEAMED the evening star;
And from embattled clouds emerging slow
Cynthia came riding on her silver car;
And hoary mountain-cliffs shone faintly from afar.

AND now the downy cheek and deepened voice
Gave dignity to Edwin's blooming prime;
And walks of wider circuit were his choice,
And vales more mild, and mountains more sublime.
One evening as he framed the careless rhyme,
It was his chance to wander far abroad,
And o'er a lonely eminence to climb,
Which heretofore his foot had never trode;
A vale appeared below, a deep retired abode.

Thither he hied, enamoured of the scene;
For rocks on rocks piled, as by magic spell,
Here scorched with lightning, there with ivy green,
Fenced from the north and east this savage dell.
Southward a mountain rose with easy swell,
Whose long, long groves eternal murmur made;
And toward the western sun a streamlet fell,
Where, through the cliffs, the eye remote surveyed
Blue hills, and glittering waves, and skies in gold arrayed.

ALONG this narrow valley you might see
The wild deer sporting on the meadow ground,
And, here and there, a solitary tree,
Or mossy stone, or rock with woodbine crowned.
Oft did the cliffs reverberate the sound
Of parted fragments tumbling from on high ;
And from the summit of that craggy mound
The perching eagle oft was heard to cry,
Or on resounding wings to shoot athwart the sky.

AND thither let the village swain repair ;
And, light of heart, the village maiden gay,
To deck with flowers her half-dishevelled hair,
And celebrate the merry morn of May.
There let the shepherd's pipe the livelong day
Fill all the grove with love's bewitching woe ;
And when mild Evening comes in mantle grey,
Let not the blooming band make haste to go.

FOR now no cloud obscures the starry void;
The yellow moonlight sleeps on all the hills;
Nor is the mind with startling sounds annoyed;
A soothing murmur the lone region fills.

AND seated on a mossy stone, he spied
An ancient man : his harp lay him beside.
A stag sprang from the pasture at his call,
And, kneeling, licked the withered hand that tied
A wreath of woodbine round his antlers tall,
And hung his lofty neck with many a flow'ret small.

ALONG yon glittering sky what glory streams !
What majesty attends Night's lovely queen !
Fair laugh our valleys in the vernal beams ;
And mountains rise, and oceans roll between,
And all conspire to beautify the scene.

DARK woods and rankling wilds, from shore to shore,
Stretch their enormous gloom; which to explore
Even Fancy trembles, in her sprightliest mood;
For there each eyeball gleams with lust of gore,
Nestles each murderous and each monstrous brood.

HE sleeps in dust, and all the Muses mourn,
He, whom each virtue fired, each grace refined,
Friend, teacher, pattern, darling of mankind !
He sleeps in dust. . . .
To heart-consuming grief resigned,
Here on his recent grave I fix my view,
And pour my bitter tears.

CPSIA information can be obtained at www.ICGtesting.com
Printed in the USA
BVOW06s1041191113

336712BV00008B/213/P